The Meaning of Life
(and AIDS Jokes)

By Tom Z
www.thetomzshow.com

Copyright Tom Z 2011

The Meaning of Life (and AIDS Jokes)
Table of contents

x - Untitled (Intro)

1) The New American Dream
2) God vs. Dave
3) How to Stop Workplace Shootings
4) Don't Vote. Seriously.
5) In 2047, Africa Will Be Made of Solid Gold
6) It's a Touchy Subject
7) Scientology is Not Real
8) The Meaning of Life
9) Aliens Suck
10) Justin Bieber Sucks
11) The Best Things in Life Are Really Expensive
12) Solving the World's Problems With Rap Lyrics: High Gas Prices
13) The Meaning of Life, Part II
14) Question For God
15) Rat-Flavored Hot Dogs Are a Metaphor For Life
16) Everything I Know, I Learned on the Street
17) Not a Pirate
18) Trying to Calculate the Amount of Money I've Spent on Alcohol in My Life
19) The Holiday Calendar According to Tom Z
20) 8 Reasons I Love McDonald's
21) My Plan to Dominate the Music Industry
22) The Meaning of Life, Part III
23) Tom Z For President
24) Black People Are the New White People
25) Smart People Are the New Idiots
26) Fuckin' Squirrels
27) I am 110 Years Ahead of My Time
28) The Meaning of Life, Part IV

29) 9 Good Things About 9/11
30) Solving the World's Problems With Rap Lyrics: Partisan Politics
31) Spoiler Alert
32) The Silver Rule
33) The Meaning of Life, Part V
34) 'I Knew I Had Hit Rock Bottom'
35) The Solution to All of the World's Problems
36) The Meaning of Life, Part VI
37) Take This Seriously

X
Untitled (Intro)

In 6th grade, I was part of my school's Enrichment Program. It was a group of roughly 15 intelligent students who administrators felt weren't being sufficiently challenged in the classroom. One period a day we would skip class and go to the Enrichment room, where we'd undertake an activity that better expanded our developing young minds. Most of the kids chose to read novels or complete extra-credit assignments. Some played board games or chess.

My friend Dan and I didn't do any of that crap. Instead, we invented a game called "Ruler Hockey." We sat at opposite ends of the room, each holding a ruler, and we tried to slap a checker across the room, past the other person. It was rude, it was disruptive, and most importantly, it didn't teach us a damn thing. This game continued for months, until one day I accidentally shanked a checker off the blackboard and hit our teacher in the face. She banned the game and insisted that we do something more productive with our time, at which point Dan and I began gambling on a bastardized version of Roulette that we created using a 20-sided die from the board game Risk.

When parent-teacher conferences finally came around, the Enrichment teacher told my parents, and I quote, "Your son has infinite potential, but zero motivation. He could be anything he wants to be, but he probably won't amount to very much."

I'll never forget that quote. In two sentences, she essentially told my parents that I was lazy, rude, useless and a disgrace to the Enrichment Program. It was the most shocking and brazen thing I've ever heard from a teacher in my life. But you know something? That bitch was right. You see, this pattern continued for the remainder of my formative years. In high school, I studied a total of 20 minutes in four years. Instead I used my TI-82 graphing calculator to cheat on tests and create video games that I played during class. My college had a beautiful, newly renovated library. I went there once. I spent the rest of my college career inventing drinking games and building a bobsled out of a shopping cart that I later crashed into the student union building. I was never that interested in applying myself, at least not in the traditional sense. It was just more fun to make jokes and fuck around. Am I lazy? Maybe. Am I inappropriate? Definitely. But this is how I expand my mind. Not through studying or assignments, but through finding new and unique ways to entertain myself. I tell stories. I come up with crazy theories. I take important world issues and make jokes about them. This is what I do.

Taking things seriously has never been my forte.

Luckily we live in a great country; one where irreverence can become a career. In 2003, I began writing an online journal. I was bored at work and needed something to occupy my time. The site started off as a bunch of drunken stories, and over time evolved to include musings on myriad topics, from music to pop culture to social issues. In 2007, I was hired to write for a music web site. That lasted a year and a half, at which point I began freelancing. All the while, I've continued updating my personal web site.

This book is a collection of articles I wrote between 2005 and 2011. Some of them come from the aforementioned personal web site, and some have never been published anywhere before. The book covers a wide range of subjects, including pop culture, society, politics, rock 'n roll, life, crazy theories, and most importantly, inappropriate jokes. I'm not an English Major or a professional wordsmith. I'm just a guy who tried to entertain himself when he wasn't challenged by his day job. I wish I could tell you that that this book is a sociopolitical analysis or a dissertation in youth culture, or that it holds a mirror up to an ever-regressing American landscape. But really, it's about one thing: Entertainment. These are the topics that occupied my mind when I was supposed to be doing something more important. I only hope that this book will entertain you. If it enriches your mind, that's great. Chances are you'll walk away confused and disoriented, feeling like you were just hit in the head by a flying checker.

So enjoy, my friends. Just don't expect too much. After all, I'm pretty fucking lazy.

-Tom Z

1
The New American Dream

Once upon a time, the American Dream was to work your way out of the bowels of poverty and up into the penthouse of success. Poor immigrants would come to America in order to get a job and feed their family. They dreamed of someday working hard enough to provide a great life for themselves and their loved ones; something that wasn't possible in their home country. Similarly, people born in America hoped that with a proper work ethic, they could accumulate wealth and ascend to a greater social status than their parents. Everyone worked their ass off to ensure that their children would have a better life than they ever did.

Well, that was then.

Now it's 2011, motherfuckers, and there's a brand new American Dream.

That dream is to get rich by doing jack-shit.

To achieve maximum success with minimal effort.

To have it all, without having to do anything.

Welcome to the 21st century.

Why do you think so many people play the lottery every day? It's not just to hold up the gas station line for 10 minutes while they scratch off 40 *Win For Life* tickets.

No, these annoying, inconsiderate, always-in-the-way assholes have a different idea, and that idea is to live The New American Dream. Millions of uneducated rednecks play the numbers every day, motivated by a burning desire to offset their laissez-faire attitude toward life with some good old fashioned random luck.

Unfortunately hitting the lotto is nearly impossible to achieve, so most people are forced to settle for a compromised version of The New American Dream, such as coasting through a lackluster job and then watching TV for 8 hours a night. It's not perfect, but it does the trick for most. Deep-down, no matter how ambitious someone may seem, all anyone really wants to do is get paid for sitting around, watching "The Simpsons" reruns and eating Doritos. If you deny this, you're either lying to yourself or you're an anti-American commie bastard. That's why movies with anti-work plots like *Office Space* and *American Beauty* have become classics. Watching these movies allows us to sit on our fat asses and do nothing, while dreaming about a life where we sit on our fat asses and do nothing. It's a double-dip of languid satisfaction, and we love it. Languid means lazy, by the way. I know you're not going to look it up in the dictionary. That would take way too much effort.

Lawsuits, workers compensation claims, "mental breakdowns," and leaves of absence are prevalent throughout our society. Why do you think people sue for slip and fall accidents? Do they really believe that walking on a recently washed floor entitles them to millions of dollars? Of course not. They see it as an easy way to make money. It's clear that Americans in this day and age will do whatever they can to get paid for doing nothing.

Just look at Paris Hilton. Since rising to national prominence, she's barely done shit. She had her own reality TV show, which means she got paid for being alive. She had a sex tape, which means she made money for fucking. Anything else she's ever needed, she just leeched off her parents. Looking at that evidence, and the fact that she's annoying as shit, it would seem that nobody would like Paris Hilton. And yet, she's arguably the biggest celebrity of the past decade. We say that we hate her, but we can't stop paying attention. Why? Because she has lived The New American Dream, and we are all envious. She is paid for living. She spends her time getting wasted, fucking around and generally having fun. "That's hot," we might say, if we weren't so jealous. I work rigorous 50-hour weeks and get almost no sleep just so I can live like Paris Hilton on the weekend. Given the option, I would trade places with her in a second. And this is coming from someone who wakes up every morning and thanks God that he doesn't have a vagina.

Of course, even Paris Hilton does something. As little as it may be, she occasionally will do stuff.

To truly achieve The New American Dream, you must find a way to do nothing — nothing at all — and be paid for it.

Which brings me to my next point:

Kevin Federline is my fucking hero.

By the time you read this, Kevin Federline will have vanished from the pop culture landscape. He will be but a footnote in the pages of retarded white trash history. But it is critical — I repeat, critical — that we do not forget him, for NOBODY embodies spirit of America in the 21st Century better than Federline.

He is The New American Dream.

I've looked up to K-Fed ever since he landed Britney Spears in the early 2000s, and over time, he has continued to elevate his game. His game being, of course, nothing. He's taken nothing to a whole new level. He's mastered the art of doing nothing, and that's why he's my idol. There's nothing I would enjoy more than having his life.

Let's look at Federline's track record. As far as we know, before marrying Spears, his only prior career was "back up dancer," which is a preposterous job since I've never heard of anyone who aspires to be a background dancer. Being a foreground dancer is stupid enough, but to actively pursue dancing in the background of a better dancer? That's insane. A true lazy man's job. Now, dancing takes some energy, and it's pretty gay, but I know I'd take any career that meant three weeks of practice and then two hours of work every 3rd night. After he started to date Britney, I would imagine that any semblance of a dancing career disappeared out the window. There he was, retired from a bogus job at the tender age of 26. His life evolved to a point where it consisted of smoking, fucking Britney Spears, doing nothing else, and living in the lap of luxury. An amazing accomplishment by any straight male's standards. Yet Federline kept raising the bar. He got engaged to Britney. Then we found out that Spears was the one who proposed. Shocking. Then, the couple had a secret spur-of-the-moment wedding, a brilliant move by Federline since it gave Britney less time to re-evaluate what she was doing. We even discovered that there was no pre-nup. No pre-nup! My God, this man is a fucking genius.

Think about this… what do we actually know about Kevin Federline? Everything we know about the guy is based on tabloid photographs. As far as we know, all he's ever done is smoke cigarettes and play with his cell phone. He always wore a white wife beater, and to the best of my knowledge, he has never spoken. Have you ever heard Federline say a single word? No, of course not, he's never been in anything besides tabloid pictures and Britney's vagina and possibly the backup dance ensemble of a boy band. The only thing Federline ever "did" was release a rap CD, but I would argue that doesn't count because the process consisted of him listening to a beat produced by someone else and talking about weed over the bassline. I'm pretty sure that's what Federline would have been doing anyways. He just decided to record it for once. That's the career of Kevin Federline. The guy's resume is a blank sheet of paper.

And yet somehow he's financially set for life and he was able to bang the biggest pop star of a generation.

The man is a true hero.

Now this is where it gets tricky. After Federline began dating Britney Spears, America witnessed Spears' descent from pop starlet to trailer trash mother of two. Some people try to demean Federline's accomplishments by pointing out that Britney turned to white trash during their relationship. I believe this strengthens Federline's case as a role model to 21st Century America. Federline is white trash, and he got Britney to become just like him. It's no different than a Jewish woman getting her man to convert to Judaism for her. Except while the Jewish woman might possess a plethora of positives, such as a great personality or feminine allure, Federline possesses a plethora of nothing, such as... umm, nothing. But despite a lack of... well, everything... Federline refused to compromise, sticking to his white trash guns while convincing Britney to follow him for 40 days and 40 nights through the wigger desert. It's a power move, and I like it.

Federline was helped greatly by the fact that we knew so little about him. I would argue this is the key to his legacy. For someone as famous as Federline was during his anti-prime, he gave almost no interviews and rarely made TV or magazine appearances that were of his own accord. Sure tabloids printed thousands of photos, but they were mostly grainy images of Federline performing a mundane task. He did have a reality show, but it was canceled after a month and I'm pretty sure no one on Earth ever saw it. Also, the show was created by Federline and Spears, who both served as executive producers. Let's put it this way: If I produced my own show, it would be called "Tom Z: The Greatest Human Ever" and the first episode would follow my quest of trying to find special pants that were large enough to fit my mammoth cock. That's not reality. We've never had any real insight into Federline's personal life. What if America had delved deeper and found out he was a really great guy? Or a good match for Brit? Or hung like a donkey? If I ever discovered that he actually had something going for him, it would ruin his whole appeal. The reason that Federline is awesome is because he seemingly landed the biggest catch on the planet despite having no redeeming qualities whatsoever. If we find out that he does in fact bring something to the table, then it just isn't the same. His reluctance to submit to the same excessive media-whoring as other celebrities, along with his JD Salinger-like disappearance in recent years, is without question the smartest thing he could have ever done.

Still, the question remains: If Federline is as great as I clearly believe he is, then why does everyone hate him? The media bashed him constantly. Late-night talk show hosts made him the butt of every joke. Trying to find a positive comment about Federline on the internet is about as easy as finding a unicorn or a leprechaun or a 20-year old from Louisiana who's not pregnant… impossible.

Why would we direct so much rage in one man's direction?

It's because we're all jealous, and we don't even know it.

We all talk ourselves into this myth of an American Dream. We have hopes and aspirations and 5-year action plans that are supposed to make us incredibly wealthy while filling our lives with joy. Or so we say. But it's a lie. Our actions clearly show that we are more interested in The New American Dream, the one where we scam just enough money from society to pay for a leather couch and a flat-screen TV so we can sit on our fat asses all day long.

The New American Dream knows no race or religion, and it certainly know no class. Whether it's a Wall Streeter betting $20 million on mysterious derivatives, or a garbage man betting $20 on the Eagles to cover, every American is trying to achieve the illustrious goal of making money without contributing anything to society.

Any person who is given the choice between working hard or getting paid to do nothing will choose the latter. Ask anyone who has collected unemployment how motivated they were to find work. Here's a hint: They weren't motivated at all, until the checks were about to dry up, at which point they magically decided it was time to get back into the workforce. Imagine if one of your company's competitors decided you were a major threat to their business, and tried to poach you away. But the company was located in a different state, and you didn't want to move. So instead, to eliminate you as a threat, the company offered to pay you the same salary and benefits if you quit your current job. You would make the same amount of money, but you wouldn't have to do anything. Wouldn't you take that deal? Since this is hypothetical, you're probably making excuses, saying things like "I need to stay busy." That's because we've been conditioned to say such things by supporters of a false American Dream. Deep down, you know you'd take that deal in a heartbeat.

Since the Family and Medical Leave Act was created in 1993, over 50 million people have taken leave from work. I'm sure much of that leave was justified, but still, 27% of those 50 million people made less than $30,000 at the time, so theoretically they would have wanted to get in some extra face-time at the office to climb the corporate ladder. According to a 2007 report, 58 million Americans binge-drink and 19.9 million use illicit drugs. One in three Americans suffers from a mental disorder, many of which are anxiety or mood-related. Why do you think that is? Do you think babies are born with anxiety disorders? Of course not. It's because the things we spend our lives doing are totally incongruent with the things we want to do. We want to hang out with friends, watch TV, go to the beach, and play video games. Basically we want to do nothing. But it costs a ton of money to be alive, so we have to get jobs and work. A ton. We don't want to work. Working sucks. Trust me. I actually had my dream job, and it was OK, but I still would have rather stayed home doing nothing.

So nobody wants to work, yet due to the outrageous cost of living, we're forced to work all the time. That's why people have nervous breakdowns, or binge-drink, or shoot meth, or join underground fight clubs, or cut themselves just to feel alive, or... well, enough about my hobbies, the point is we all hate work and would rather get paid for nothing.

There is one caveat, which is the key to understanding our anger over do-nothing celebrities. While we all hope desperately to achieve The New American Dream, we only want it for ourselves. That's the dirty little secret of The New American Dream. When someone else finds a way to make tons of money with minimal effort, we hate that person. We become filled with a jealousy so massive that it could barely fit inside Britney Spears' vagina.

Which brings us back to Federline. He'll always draw the ire of many, but to me, he will forever remain a real American hero, like George Washington or Hulk Hogan. He accomplished what each of us strives for every single day of our lives. How a man of such ill repute amassed a fortune and bedded the premier pop star of our time with zero effort is a mystery greater than the existence of mankind. Federline is a beacon of light, giving hope to every sub-par male that they too can land a rich, gorgeous and talented woman despite having no noticeable talent or ambition. He is The New American Dream. There's a little bit of us in Kevin Federline, and there's a whole lot of Federline in each of us. If you hate Kevin Federline, you hate America. Shame on you, anonymous Internet commenters.

2
God vs. Dave

I'd like to talk about a great deity.

In fact, some might call him the greatest deity.

Millions around the globe worship him. He reigns over his many followers, spreading a message of love and compassion. He gives light to those in their darkest hour. He is responsible for some of the most cherished writings in history. People base their entire lives around him, and are willing to defend his teachings to the death. He created mankind and helped Moses part the Red Sea.

That's right… I'm talking about Dave Matthews.

OK, so he didn't do that last thing, but have you heard "Grey Street?" That song fuckin' rocks, man!

You're probably thinking, "How dare you compare God with Dave?" Even though 'Dave' is your good buddy, hence why you refer to him by his first name only, you still don't understand how a singer/songwriter can compare to the all-knowing entity that is God.

Well, I'm here to tell you, they aren't that different. Get ready, cause this is about to get heavy.

It begins with the followers. God and Dave both have them, in great numbers. Christianity is the most popular religion on Earth, with an influence stretching to all corners of the globe. Christianity is certainly more popular than the Dave Matthews Band, but let's not be fooled: Dave has legions of followers himself.

Just as the typical Sunday mass is attended by casual Christians and devoted patrons alike, the average DMB crowd includes diehard fans, along with a bunch of people who just think that "Tripping Billies" rules. Many people at church may be going through the motions, pretending to care, while their true intentions are simply to put on a show for their neighbors. Likewise, a lot of people go to Dave Matthews shows to get drunk. However, whether attending a sermon or a Dave concert, one thing is certain: You'll find *plenty* of devout followers. They come to have their lives transformed by the man whom they worship. It is a brief moment of enlightenment in their otherwise murky lives. Some may go to church to hear remarkable sermons or listen to killer hymnal tunes, but we know that a lot of people are there for the message. They want to hear the Word of the Lord. Similarly, for many fans, the love of Dave Matthews goes well beyond the music. In their mind it is often one of the few things that makes life worth living. Just as God can get people through their moments of confusion and doubt, Dave can guide his listeners through troublesome relationships and help them re-evaluate what is truly important in their lives. There is solace to be found in the lyrics of "The Space Between," just as there is solace to be found in the book of Genesis.

Perhaps the biggest similarity between God and Dave — or as I call them, God and Super-God — is their writings. God, of course, has the Bible, while Dave has his lyrics. The Bible teaches many incredible lessons, such as "love thy neighbor" and the story of David and Goliath. Dave has also given us some gems, such as "If you hold on too tight to what you think is your thing, you may find you're missing all the rest." Both rely heavily on storytelling; their stories seem implausible from a factual standpoint but contain important underlying messages. Honestly, what sounds less realistic: A man talking to a snake, or a bunch of ants marching? If someone was unfamiliar with both Christianity and Dave Matthews, I doubt they'd be able to determine which of those stories came from the Bible and which came from *Under the Table and Dreaming*. Both stories are ridiculous taken at face value, but both offer valuable lessons for the avid listener to come away with. And that's the whole point.

Neither group, Christians nor Dave fans, are hesitant about spreading the word of their Savior. For each time a representative of the Church of Latter Day Saints has knocked on my door, there has been a separate moment in my life where someone told me how I "totally need to listen to the Dave bootleg from night two in Saratoga" because "he jams out friggin' forever at the end of #41, bro."

On the flip side, both have detractors. Many atheists are quite vocal in disavowing the existence of God, claiming that religion is nothing more than a crutch for the weak. Similarly, there are plenty of Dave-eists out there; critics who hate Dave's music, his fans, and what his band represents in the pop culture landscape. Neither group is quiet about their displeasures with God/Dave.

You probably think I'm joking around. But really, what's the difference between God and Dave?

Sure, they have different back stories. One created the Earth and sent his only son to be born of the Virgin Mary and crucified for the sins of all mankind. The other was a bartender that started a band with an unoriginal name in his spare time and slowly gained a following in Virginia.

But from a cultural standpoint, they have a lot in common. Both have huge numbers of intensely devoted fans. Both are worshipped. Both have insightful writings that may or may not be based on fact. Both provide comfort in times of sorrow and are praised during periods of joy. Both can provoke massive fits of outrage or inspire life affirming epiphanies. Both are better when you funnel 18 beers in the parking lot beforehand.

You see what I'm getting at. Let's say two men were to suffer similar tragedies on the same day. One, a lifelong Christian, rushes to church to pray for better days. The other, a diehard Dave fan, sits at home alone and listens to *Crash* while mourning. Would these not both be suitable methods for dealing with grief? Wouldn't each man be dealing with tragedy in a manner that best suits him, gaining comfort from an important and familiar presence? Wouldn't both be seeking the guidance of a wise sage in their time of need?

Then why do we look at people who frequent church as saints, and people who tour with Dave Matthews as burnouts? God can get people through the hard times, but so can Dave. God can be there for the good times, but so can Dave. Both God fans and Dave fans find solace in their respective leaders, and consider them a precious and necessary part of their lives.

So, if some people get the same value out of Dave that others do out of God, then why don't we start to appreciate his music as a unique, alternative form of religion?

Maybe it's because Dave Matthews sucks. But you get my point.

3
How to Stop Workplace Shootings

As you know, there has been a rash of workplace shootings lately. American employees, fed up with their stressful jobs and insufficient wages, are going into work armed to the teeth and causing massive chaos. Each workplace gunman blames a new enemy — the government, taxes, racism, a jerk boss — but the results are always the same. Innocent people dead or wounded, and a shooter who kills himself before the police even arrive. It's a terrible tragedy every time something like this happens.

Luckily, I have a solution.

I think we can decrease the number of workplace shootings with one simple step.

How you ask? It's easy.

First we have to ask ourselves this question: Why do people shoot up a public place? I believe they do it for attention. If they were tired of life, they would just kill themselves. Take some pills, jump off a bridge, lock yourself in a closet with a Taylor Swift CD on loop until you gouge your own heart out... whatever floats your boat. Kurt Cobain was sick of life. He didn't storm into a Gold's Gym and light the place up. When you're taking out innocent lives before turning the gun on yourself, you're trying to make people notice you. These gunmen are trying to enact revenge against their bosses, ex-lovers, the popular clique, and anyone else they despise. That revenge fantasy goes hand-in-hand with the attention seeking. A sane person who hates their boss looks for another job. They realize it's a bad situation and they get out. Someone who's fed up with a spouse gets a divorce. A child who hates their school focuses on achieving good grades and then goes to college somewhere far, far away. Anyone who believes it is their responsibility to enact a God-like revenge is clearly starved for attention. When you read about any of these incidents, you can see the clues all over the place.

"I was a victim..."

"I gave them the justice they deserved..."

"He shot at the popular kids..."

Workplace (and schoolplace) shooters feel that they've been dealt a bad hand in life. They could overcome this by having a personality or by accomplishing something, but since they're all crazy losers with no redeeming qualities, they get the attention they've been seeking the only way they know how... by going into a crowded building with a gun. Of course the media plays right into their plan by covering the shootings ad nauseum.

Assuming my theory is correct and gunmen are doing it for the publicity, there's an easy way to stop them. We make sure that the publicity people get for shooting up a business is the kind of publicity that no one would ever want to have.

That's right... we call them a pedophile.

Yes, from now on, whenever someone shoots up a crowded place, every news story should be required to include at least one line saying that the gunman was an alleged child molester. The stories would read something like this...

Charles Stevenson, 28, of Pittsburgh, PA, stormed into a Bally's Fitness Center on Main Street at 9:00 this morning and began shooting an AK-47 at gym members. Nine people were killed, including Stevenson, who eventually turned the gun on himself. Seven others were wounded. Stevenson, a former employee of the gym, is believed to have had a major argument with the owner of the club two days prior. Friends say Stevenson had been acting erratically for weeks.

Stevenson is also allegedly a pedophile.

Or how about this...

John Montgomery, 37, of Utica, NY, walked into a Wegman's grocery store at 4:00PM yesterday with two pistols. Montgomery opened fire in the direction of the customer service counter, then turned his aim towards cashiers and finally toward store customers. The ordeal lasted 32 minutes and ended when Montgomery took his own life during a stand-off with police. Fourteen people are dead, and 3 others are wounded.

Montgomery was allegedly upset after a cashier refused to accept an expired coupon for Campbell's Soup. Also, Montgomery is allegedly a toucher. Several unidentified sources confirmed that he enjoyed touching little boys.

Or this...

Jake Williams, 42, of Alexandria, VA, shot 37 people inside a Sonic this morning. Also, I heard the dude loves molesting children. I mean, allegedly, this guy is an unchecked sexual deviant satiated only by the supple feel of a child's genitals. Tons of people said so. Trust us. Everyone in Alexandria knows Jake Williams LOVES fucking kids.

You might be questioning the legality of my method, but trust me, it's fine. I've worked in journalism. As long as you put words like "allegedly" or "reportedly" at the beginning of the sentence, you can say anything. You want to say some dude likes grabbing kids' behinds? No problem. Just say he "allegedly loves grabbing child ass." Legally you're off the hook and everyone who reads it will believe that your accusation is true. Plus, even if it's ethically wrong, it doesn't matter, because who's going to come to the defense of a child-molesting mass murderer? No one. Would you defend a murdering pedophile? Of course not. That's worse than defending a terrorist. At least with the terrorists you can make up some weak argument about America's immoral smut peddling or the Kardashians. With kiddie-rapist gunmen, you got nothing.

Do this for one year, and I promise you will never see a massive workplace shooting again. Gunmen want the media to talk about the injustices they faced, not the crotches they touched. They want to be a martyr, not a baby rapist. Copycat killings and attention-seekers would disappear forever, and only the craziest

0.00000000000000000001% would ever even consider shooting up a public place again. This type of crime would be virtually erased from our society. Plus it would raise a lot of awareness about pedophilia. It's really a win-win.

4
Don't Vote. Seriously.

Very soon, we'll be faced with another Presidential election. Like every Presidential election, it will be declared "the most important election of our lifetime" by the overzealous media. As the next election draws nearer and nearer, you're going to hear a lot of talk about how important voting is. I'm sure you're familiar with past campaigns such as "Vote or Die," "Choose or Lose," and "Rock the Vote," that tried to encourage people to get out and vote. The next election will be no different. Surely we'll witness the most intense and far-reaching voter registration campaign our country has ever seen. You'll be inundated with information about the importance of voting, and how voting is one of your civic duties.

I'm here to offer a slightly different take:

Don't vote.

Seriously.

Now before you jump to conclusions or start screaming about how it's our duty as an American to vote, hear me out...

Voting is an incredibly important responsibility. The Presidents we choose not only rule this country, but become de facto leaders for the entire world. Furthermore, each subsequent President faces more turmoil, more vitriol, and more difficult and nuanced predicaments than any of his (or her) predecessors. We live in a time of economic and social crisis. It's an age of terrorism and war, where the reputation and power of the United States is constantly eroding.

Living in a Democracy means that the people choose the leaders. That means all of the power of this great nation lies with you.

You're not worthy of that responsibility.

Why? Because you're an idiot.

Don't take that personally. I don't mean you're Corky from "Life Goes On" retarded or anything. I just mean that you lack the necessary information to cast an intelligent vote. Or maybe you don't. Maybe you have all the facts, and you're ready to get out and rock the vote next election. If so, hey, congratulations. You're part of a vast, vast minority in this country that knows what they're doing. The U.S. has about 300 million citizens, and of those, 16 are qualified to vote. Alright, so I made that number up, but seriously, it's really low. Even if it's half, which I think is extremely generous, that means there are a ton of unqualified people out there tainting the voting pool every election.

Each election, a lot of Americans don't vote.

That, my friends, is a good thing.

I have a friend, who shall remain nameless. Before the 2008 election, she told me she was originally planning to vote for Barack Obama, but after Obama wore a few ugly ties, she began thinking about changing her vote. This is a girl who based her vote on a candidate's choice of ties. Her vote counts exactly the same as yours.

A few years ago, Britney Spears gave an interview in which she said, "I love seeing my fans overseas, especially in Canada." Britney Spears gets to vote each November, and her vote counts exactly the same as every other American's. James Carville is a political mastermind who might know more about politics than anyone on Earth, but his vote will count exactly the same as Britney Spears'.

I once heard a story of someone voting for John Kerry because Ben Affleck said to. I know someone who said they'll always vote Republican regardless of candidate because they're anti-abortion, and when I asked them if they'd still vote Republican even if Hitler were running for the party, they just shrugged and said "I don't know."

We're going out of our way to get these people to vote?

I know what you're thinking: These are extreme examples, and these people are idiots. That's where you're wrong. All of the people mentioned in the previous examples are normal people of average to above-average intelligence. Well, except for Britney Spears. Still, you think you're better or smarter than them. Maybe, but most people aren't. Two-thirds of people can't find Iraq on a map; 33% can't find Louisiana. There are people that don't even know who the current President is. How that's possible is beyond me, but it's true.

OK, so we all know there are some true idiots out there, and you're light years beyond them… but how much did you *really* know about the 2008 election? Can you tell me where Barack Obama stands on various issues without looking it up on Google? Can you name 4 things that John McCain wanted to accomplish if he was elected? Can you tell me your stance on anything without copying something you heard on "The Daily Show" or "Fox News?"

I don't think you can. Well, maybe YOU can, because if you're reading this you're obviously really smart. But can everyone in this country be trusted with a vote?

Every election involves many important issues. All of these issues require a complex examination. There are no easy answers. Solutions vary from week to week as the world changes and new circumstances arise. When it comes to foreign and domestic policy, nothing is black and white. To understand politics requires not only a certain initial mental capacity; it requires that you pay constant attention as well.

Yet if you watch the news, all you hear about are ancillary issues. Here are some of the things the average citizen was concerned about prior to the '08 election: John McCain's age, something Barack Obama's minister once said, some quote Obama's wife said awhile back, whether McCain's wife was addicted to pills... the list of pseudo-issues goes on and on.

The point is this: Once you set aside people with unwavering party allegiances, the rest of this nation — the voters who ultimately decide every election — almost always choose their leaders based on a gut feeling. Unless we're incredibly knowledgeable about politics, unless we've spent countless hours studying the positions and policies of ALL candidates, unless we have an in-depth knowledge of all the issues and what it will take to solve them, unless we're unbiased and free from personal agendas or vendettas, then our gut feeling is going to be wrong. You could pick the better person, but if you didn't pick them for the right reasons, it's not Democracy, it's luck. The average person who goes to a voting booth is like a blindfolded kid swatting at a piñata at a Cinco de Mayo party. You might get some candy, but you also might whack Uncle Jimmy in the testicles with a baseball bat. Is that how we should choose the most powerful man on the planet? You might as well put two bowls of cat food on a table, with one candidate's name on each, and let a kitten decide.

What we need is a pre-voting test. Everyone who wants to vote should be forced to take a test when registering. People who score well enough and know what they're doing get one vote. Someone with an exceptional knowledge of our country and politics — for example, James Carville — gets two votes. People who cast their votes based on wardrobes, celebrity advice, or any other stupid reason get zero. People who can't name the President get shipped off to Cuba on a raft. And not the nice part of Cuba, either. The bad part.

Unfortunately, in a Democracy we have to treat everyone as equal, even when they're not, so that will never happen. Therefore, the next best and most honorable thing you can do as a voter is to admit when you don't know shit, and concede that you shouldn't vote. Take a self inventory, then instead of voting, sit on your ass and watch a rerun of the 1995 Rose Bowl on ESPN Classic. Because dammit, that's something you *are* qualified to do!

This isn't about preventing anyone from voting. I would never suggest that. This is about giving up the quest to make every single person vote. This is about encouraging the unqualified to take some personal responsibility and realize that they shouldn't be in a voting booth. Regardless of what the activists tell you, there's no shame in not voting. It's a hell of a lot tougher to admit your limitations and skip the election than to be a lemming and cast an uneducated vote because it's the "right" thing to do.

Anyone can claim that his or her vote matters.

It takes a real man or woman to admit their vote doesn't mean dick.

If you're not educated about politics, don't vote. If you're unaware of the issues, don't vote. If you have no strong feelings about either candidate, don't vote. If you're voting for someone you don't care about simply because he's the lesser of two evils, don't vote. If you're voting for someone because of gender or race, don't vote. If your candidate lost the primary and you're simply voting for whoever won the nomination for that party, don't vote. If you're voting for someone because they're taller or better looking than the other guy, don't vote. If you're voting because someone told you "if you don't vote, you can't complain," don't vote (and then complain anyways)! If you're voting for someone because your favorite celebrity endorses them, for God's sake, DON'T VOTE!

ONLY YOU HAVE THE POWER TO NOT VOTE IN THE NEXT ELECTION!!!

Those of you who are well-educated, understand the political process, realize what each candidate brings to the table, and then make a rational decision based on the information at hand, good for you. Enjoy casting your vote in November.

The rest of us, let's tell the boss we're going to vote, go to Starbucks and surf the Internet for cat videos instead. It's better for society, and let's be honest, we'll enjoy it way more.

5
In 2047, Africa Will Be Made of Solid Gold

In 10,500 BC, the continent of Africa was a fertile valley, perfect for crop growth. But then, due to climate shifts, Africa began to dry out. The resulting deserts were terrible for farming, and a crop shortage ensued. Colonization of the continent over the past thousand years has caused a great deal of territorialism and civil war. What's more, the recent spread of HIV/AIDS has left Africa crippled. Modern Africa is defined by poverty, disease, and war. Times are tough. At the same time, the rest of the world seems callous to this fact. Americans especially seem to ignore the plight of Africa, opting instead for their high-definition televisions and Grand Slam Breakfasts. Sure, foreign governments and international organizations have tried to help Africa, but nothing seems to work.

And that's why musicians had to step in.

With Africa in a state of disarray, it was important for the likes of Bono and Alicia Keys to step up to the plate and inspire hope. World leaders might get slowed down by politics and red tape, but celebrities have instant access to the people. Inspire the people, and only then can you see change. In fact, with the way musicians have been promoting Africa lately, it's only a matter of time until things turn around for that continent.

We're still in the early part of the 21 century, and although things may look bleak now, a simple extrapolation of the timeline shows that Africa is in for a bright future. And it's all thanks to musicians.

Let's take a look...

1985 - Held on July 13th, Bob Geldorf's massive Live Aid rock concerts were seen by 1.5 billion people worldwide, raising awareness of the long-suffering continent. Millions of dollars are raised. Legendary singer Bob Dylan — known for his social activism — suggests we used a portion of the money raised to help farmers in America. He is staunchly criticized by both Geldorf and the media.

1995 - The popular movie *Ace Ventura: When Nature Calls* takes place in Africa. This does little for the continent's survival; however, it does provide society with the hilarious line, "Pretty hot in these rhinos."

2004 - The United States falls behind Japan and China in trade. The U.S., which was also a leader in the field of education, continues to slip in that regard as well. Somewhere, a young Chinese boy calls an American boy a "retard," and instead of replying with a witty remark like, "Did you mean to call me a 'Letald?,'" the American boy is left speechless.

2005 - Twenty years after the fact, the effects of Live Aid are still unclear. U2 singer Bono goes on "Meet the Press" to talk about Africa, in what will become a recurring trend. Bono mentions that corruption, not poverty or starvation, is Africa's biggest problem. Bono goes on to spend much of his time working in politics, completely resisting the urge to write good music in the process. Seriously, that "Vertigo" song sucks. In tragic news, Hurricane Katrina strikes the city of New Orleans, leaving the city destroyed and thousands homeless. The U.S. government promises to fix the situation ASAP.

2007 - Bono pushes the nation of Germany to send financial aid to Africa in early 2007. Around this same time, Pete Wentz of Fall Out Boy travels to Uganda to record a video and take part in a protest against the mistreatment of Ugandan refugees. 14 year old Ugandan girls turn out in record numbers. The magazine *Vanity Fair* prints 20 different covers of a special "Africa" issue, each one featuring a different celebrity or musician. Many stars of the music world, including Jay-Z, Alicia Keys and — of course — Bono, are photographed for the various covers. In July, Al Gore's Live Earth concert series is held to a massive audience across the globe. Though they are meant to raise awareness for global warming, the concerts unintentionally spark more interest in human rights issues, especially the situation in Africa. Money is donated in record numbers to the continent as people continue to destroy the environment at will. Meanwhile, United States President George W. Bush asks for $30 billion to fight AIDS in Africa. In response, the city of New Orleans releases a statement reading, "Hi... still here."

November 2011 - Hollaback Mobile, a new cell phone company, donates proceeds from its new campaign ("Holla at Rwanda") to African relief. Christina Aguilera acts as the face and breasts of the campaign. Assisted by the support of various other musicians, Africans begin to take rudimentary steps toward a better life. Many Africans can now afford the basics, such as food and clothing, and condoms are distributed, greatly reducing the spread of HIV/AIDS.

August 2012 - Money continues to pour in. Africans are now able to afford basic housing and filtered water. Bono holds a summit in London to announce that, "even though we have made great strides in Africa, the job is not even close to finished." A month later, U2 releases a crappy CD.

May 2013 - Because of the country's dependence on foreign oil, many U.S. citizens are going broke paying for gasoline, which is now $14 a gallon. Though hybrid cars are readily available, no one buys them because they're considered really lame. The people of New Orleans completely give up and just start trading in their cars for boats. Non-hybrid boats, of course.

July 2014 - The American educational system slips a little more, putting it just below Indonesia in the ranks. Meanwhile, royalties from a new album called *Clap For Africa* — a collection of Eric Clapton covers — provides Africa with the money to afford more schools and roadways. African manufacturers decide to sharply increase their production of low-cost, electric-powered vehicles. Around the same time, riots break out in the American city of Detroit, causing chaos and leaving the city uninhabitable.

October 2015 - It is discovered that Sally Struthers was embezzling funds, which finally explains why her "Save Africa" commercials were on all the time and yet had no effect whatsoever. Millions of dollars are recovered and sent to the continent. With all of its people's basic needs taken care of, African officials begin to strategically loan out and invest the money. Back in America, the Chicago Cubs win the World Series for the first time in 106 years, and during the celebration, the entire city of Chicago is accidentally burned to the ground.

February 2016 - Bono, Chester Bennington of Linkin Park (which is now a contemporary jazz band), and uber-political activist Miley Cyrus hold a telethon for Africa. Bono explains, "even though the seeds have been planted and have started to grow, they still need water to become a full-bloomed flower." Americans, who currently read at a 4th grade level, nod and write checks. The telethon, which included a much-talked-about appearance from a coked-out Dakota Fanning, receives the best Internet TV ratings of the year, barely edging out the country's most popular game show, "Guess Which Hand the Coin Is In." A month later, U2 releases another crappy CD.

January 2022 - After years where it seemed like no progress was being made, Africa hits a jackpot in the stock market with all its previously invested money. The continent can now afford luxuries such as parks, stadiums, and museums. AIDS is virtually non-existent, and those few people that do contract the disease receive a blessing when Magic Johnson donates the cure during a telethon.

September 2024 - After spending off all its tax money on a new baseball stadium, the American city of Houston goes bankrupt and dissolves. Similar scenarios occur in Pittsburgh, St. Louis, and Denver.

March 2025 - An album called *AfriCabo Wabo* — a collection of Sammy Hagar covers — donates proceeds towards African relief. Bono issues the following statement: "We must continue to look after Africa. We've watched it burst through its cocoon and evolve into a fully-grown butterfly. And now that it is spreading its wings and leaving the nest, we must continue to support it in its eternal journey, so that it is not caught in the net of relapse and placed into the jar of despair." Americans nod, write checks, and go back to watching the popular game show "How Many Fingers Am I Holding Up?" A month later, U2 releases a new CD. It's not bad, but because of his activism, Bono failed to realize that CDs had gone extinct 12 years earlier. Meanwhile, the entire city of New Orleans, which has since relocated to Birmingham, Alabama, is destroyed by a tornado. The government promises to fix the situation ASAP.

October 2028 - Thanks to a strange climate shift brought on by hairspray containers, for the first time in 10,000 years, Africa is a fertile valley again, while the Western Hemisphere has begun to dry up into a desert-like state. African farmland, which is managed by robots, is incredible. Africans are not only self-sufficient, but they are able to provide for the entire continent of Asia as well. Thanks to its superior athlete training facilities, Africa dominates the 2028 Olympics and gains every endorsement known to man. The money goes toward providing each citizen with a hoverboard, after African officials watch a copy of *Back to the Future* and think, "why didn't America make this happen already?"

December 2031 - Crime in America has risen to astronomical levels. Murder rates are especially out of hand. Many European experts — America no longer has experts — blame the popular rap song, "Stop Rattin' and Start Muthafuckin' Shootin'" by the artist Yung Assazzin.

The entire city of Baltimore is murdered. As an act of solidarity, the African government removes thousands of ancient tribal shields from its museums and sends them to America for protection.

April 2034 - Bono, Ricky Martin (now a senator from Florida), and Supreme Court Justice Jenna Jameson hold a press conference for African relief. Bono makes the following statement: "Even though Africa has surpassed both America and Europe as a society, it is important that we continue to support the continent. The only way we can improve our countries is by improving our souls, and the only way we can improve our souls is to show the goodness of our hearts through charitable donation." Americans nod, write checks, reapply their Tyson Chicken-flavored feeding tubes, and turn back to the popular game show "Is This a Man or a Kitten?" A month later, U2 releases a CD with absolutely nothing on it.

January 2038 - Inspired by Bono's words, but too lazy to act on them for 4 years, Americans go out in record numbers to buy the album *A Nickel and a Creed: Doing What We Can to Support Africa*. The album — a collection of Nickelback and Creed covers — costs only a nickel. Even though America recently decided to make its nickels out of solid gold in order to be as flashy as possible, they still have $1/1,000^{th}$ the monetary value of the African penny due to the anemic state of the American economy. (The U.S. President recently sent most of the country's printed currency to a Nigerian prince after receiving an urgent email.) Africa accepts this gift of gold coins as a show of good faith. Meanwhile, the city of New Orleaningham, which has relocated to Lexington, Kentucky, is destroyed by a 97-

foot tall, chemically-enhanced cockroach. The cockroach continues its rampage through much of the Midwest. The government promises to take care of the cockroach ASAP.

November 2042 - African scientists, regarded as the best in the world, develop the technology that allows humans to fly. A small chip is installed in each African citizen's arm that, in addition to the powers of flight, allows them all of the same abilities as the chick in *Terminator 3*. Meanwhile, in the American city of Las Vegas, a man loses $400 on one hand of blackjack, snaps, chokes the dealer, and then goes on a massive killing spree that leaves everyone in the entire state of Nevada and half of Utah dead.

June 2047 - Always proactive, Africa decides to take the stockpile of America's gold nickels and melt them down, then coat the entire continent with liquid gold. After the process is complete, Africa is made of solid gold, with 50-foot golden walls going around the entire continent. Angelina Jolie's 32 adopted African children ask their mom if they can go back home.

August 2050 - Pollution proves deadly, as the polar icecaps melt and unleash a massive tidal wave throughout the Atlantic and Pacific Oceans. The Pacific tidal wave blankets America's west coast, leaving everything west of the Rocky Mountains under water. The Atlantic tidal wave heads directly at Africa. However, it bounces off Africa's 50-foot solid gold wall and heads back at America with twice its original velocity. The waves engulf America's east coast, all the way to the Mississippi River. New York, Boston, Miami and all other major eastern cities are lost. The city of New

Orlexingtoninham, which has recently relocated to Cincinnati, is totally flooded. The government says, "bahhdfldahf ahghaldgkd ndal;fjda hhdka lahdldahgd." The government is now under water; that loosely translates to "we'll take care of it ASAP." All surviving Americans are forced to go underground to survive, except for born-again Christians and death metal fans, both of whom embrace the pending apocalypse.

*****

2100 - An American, who moved to Europe after surviving the Great Flood of 2050, takes a vacation to Africa's Paradise Coast (formerly known as Somalia). While staying in his 6-star resort on a beach with sand made of tiny platinum shards, he turns on the TV. TVs now exist in thin air and can be turned on using the mind. A commercial comes on, featuring a woman holding a dying child.

A narrator reads the following message:

"For just pennies a day, you can help save this impoverished American boy's life. Each day, thousands of Americans die due to illness, starvation, and disease. They can't even afford the basic necessities like food and water. It's a life that you couldn't possibly comprehend. But you can make a difference. Won't you please donate?"

The man sheds a single tear, then teleports down to the beach.

6
It's A Touchy Subject

So you just finished reading the previous chapter on Africa, and you're probably feeling a little uncomfortable. Even though that chapter was a satirical look at global charity, meant to call into question America's responsibility for upholding the well being of other nations at a time when we face our own unique struggles, your mind no doubt leapt to the issue of race. America is a wealthy country ruled predominantly by white men, built upon slave labor. Africa, on the other hand, is an impoverished nation of mostly black people, one whose residents were captured and sold into slavery for centuries. To compare America and Africa in any way is to summon up the difficult topic of race.

It seems every week in this country there's another big news story that involves race. Whether it's a news report about white cops getting overly physical with black suspects, a protest against affirmative action, or a story about inner city gang violence, race permeates the headlines.

Now, I don't have the answers to any of these problems.

What I do know is this: Any time race comes into the picture, things get a little sticky.

We like to think we've come a long way since the 1950s, but there's still a good deal of racial tension in our country. As a white guy, I'm hesitant to say *anything* about race, because I fear that my words could be misinterpreted so easily. Race is such a touchy subject that it feels like we're all constantly walking on eggshells. That's why I have a strict policy to never say anything bad about a black person under any circumstances. In fact, I won't even say anything that could be considered remotely controversial. Actually, just to be safe, I don't like to talk about black people at all. Or to them. I know how easily words can be misinterpreted, so I make sure that I never say a word to a black person ever. I also prefer not to look at them, just in case my look is misinterpreted as some bigoted glance. So whenever a black guy walks by me on the street and smiles or says hello, I immediately look away, then scoff and mutter "my God," in order to display my displeasure with the social stigmas that create these horrible barriers between the races. Then I usually say something to the effect of "there goes the neighborhood," because I think it's unfortunate that I live in a neighborhood where black and white people can't live in harmony. Then I duck my head straight down and hustle away as quickly as possible. Cause, you know, I don't want anyone to think I'm racist.

7
Scientology is Not Real

There are few things that all Americans can agree on, but one opinion that seems fairly unanimous is that Scientology is insane. Everyone who isn't a Scientologist, regardless of their religion, seems to agree that Scientology makes absolutely no sense, that it's a scam, and that its believers are batshit crazy.

I think people are threatened by Scientology because it seems to be the only religion that involves effort. You have to give up alcohol and pills, and you have to work to ascend levels and achieve maximum enlightenment. In other religions you just have to have faith; you don't actually have to DO anything.

Scientology might be crazy if it was a real religion, but I'm here to tell you that it's not.

I am positive that Scientology is a trick that rich people are playing on the rest of us.

Have you ever met a Scientologist? Of course not. They don't exist in real life. The only followers of Scientology are the rich and famous. When I think of Christianity, I think of devout Christians visiting the Vatican. Mention Islam and I think of believers praying toward Mecca. If it's Buddhism we're discussing, my mind leaps to visions of pacifists striving for enlightenment. Or, if you want to be cynical about it, Christianity makes me think of priests molesting children, Islam makes me think of terrorists, and Buddhism makes me think about shoeless dudes with weird facial hair and B.O. doing yoga. Either way, these religions make me think of regular people.

But mention Scientology, and I think of Tom Cruise.

I don't think about average, everyday Scientologists, because they don't exist. That's how I know the religion is an act. It's nothing but a play for rich actors. The aliens are their co-stars and the planet Earth is their stage.

Why go through all that effort for a religion that's not real?

Simple.

Boredom.

I think that one day Tom Cruise and John Travolta were bored and they started talking.

Cruise said, "We've provided joy to millions, we've married beautiful women, we're world-famous, and we've starred in critically acclaimed films. What can we do to entertain ourselves now?"

Then Travolta was like, "What if we embrace a fake religion and see if we can get people to believe it's real?"

And that's how Scientology became the force it is today.

Think about it. If you're Tom Cruise, there's nothing left to accomplish on the silver screen. When you've done *Risky Business*, *Top Gun*, *Cocktail*, *Days of Thunder*, *Jerry Maguire*, *Minority Report*, and 9,000 other films, there's not a script in Hollywood that piques your interest anymore. It's all been done. You think Travolta wants to star in *Face/Off 2*? Hell no. That's why, if you're these stars, you have to take your acting skills to a new level. What is Scientology if not the role of a lifetime? It's a chance for Cruise to perform forever, in front of the whole planet. Getting people to believe you're into Scientology is a million times harder than getting them to believe you're a bartender. I'll admit, it's an inspiring performance, and I appreciate Tom Cruise's passion for the role, but I'm not buying the act.

There's also the fact that Scientology was created by a science fiction writer, L. Ron Hubbard, in 1952. A writer. Just as Cruise got bored of acting, Hubbard probably got bored of the publishing industry and wanted to take his gift for creation to a different level. He wanted to come up with a story that was larger than life, and that reached a global audience. So he invented Scientology. Remember, this was in the 1950s, before the Internet. Back then, religious fanaticism was the best way to reach a mass audience. Today, he'd just go on Twitter.

I have to admit, he came up with a pretty good story. If you examine the tenets of Scientology, it sort of resembles a send-up of more traditional religions. Let's say you're a writer looking to create a religion that's ridiculous, yet will still be believed by some people. Scientology is exactly the kind of thing you'd come up with. It's like a satire of religion. It's got the Supreme Being, it's got the inner spirits, it has the morality clause, and it even has the pointless traditions. It's religion, but bigger and wackier. Scientology is to religions what *Scary Movie* is to horror films.

I'll give the Scientologists credit. They came up with a good gag and they've been able to keep a straight face while pulling this prank on the world. Unfortunately it's all bogus. Cruise doesn't believe in this crap. He's drinking a Heineken and popping a Vicodin right now, laughing at all us peons who criticize Scientology. We're falling for his master plan.

Well, I won't be a pawn in his game. I think Scientology is awesome. And it makes perfect sense, too. If I had to choose one religion as the perfect religion, it would definitely be Scientology. All hail my new alien overlord Xenu!

8
The Meaning of Life

Growing up, my grandfather Joe was an inspiration to me. My three other grandparents had all been killed in (separate) car accidents, so he was the only remaining elder in my life. Oh sure, I had my parents, but sometimes as a child you spend so much time arguing with your parents and fighting with them over stupid issues that you aren't capable of stepping back and absorbing the knowledge they have to offer. On the other hand, Grandpa Joe never had to worry about disciplining me, so he was able to spend time spoiling me and passing along precious nuggets of wisdom. My grandfather was both a source of constant inspiration as well as a fountain of unending knowledge.

Some people only see their grandparents on holidays or at the occasional family get-together, but such was not the case for me. Grandpa Joe and I spent a ton of time together. When I was just a small child, I used to help him with yard work, and then we would always go inside and play a game of chess (or two). As he taught me how to use a knight advantageously, he also taught me dozens of other important life lessons. It was from him that I learned most of the wisdom and lessons that shaped me into the person I am today. My grandfather was not only a great friend; he was my hero.

Sadly, when I was 18 years old, my grandfather was diagnosed with pancreatic cancer. He fought the disease tooth and nail, but eventually it spread to other organs and began to slowly wear down his body. He passed away a year and a half later. On his final day, I went to visit him in the hospital for what would be the last time. I can still remember the moment vividly. As I sat there watching a story about the Bosnian civil war on the evening news, my grandfather summoned for me to move closer. He said to me, "I have something very important to tell you." I leaned in close and he began to whisper in my ear.

For as long as I live, I'll never forget what he said:

"Tom, first, I just want to say that spending time with you over these past 19 years has been one of the best and most fulfilling things in my entire life. I know I tried to teach you a lot of stuff when you were younger. Some of it was probably good advice, and some of it was probably not that great. Well, what I'm about to tell you is hands down the most important lesson I could ever wish to share with you. You're a great kid, and I can tell you're going to go on to big things. But if you want to have an amazing and truly fulfilling life, the most important thing you could ever know is…"

Oh, by the way, before I continue with this story, did anyone see those pictures of Lindsay Lohan from the other day? Oh man! Is it just me or does she look totally pregnant? Do you think she's faking it? She's wearing one of those maternity shirts, but those are kinda the style right now, ya know? I wouldn't be surprised if she's faking though. She's such a publicity whore! Where's her mother at?!? I know this girl who hung out with her once, and she told me that Lindsay is a total bitch! But what if it's true? Isn't she supposed to be a lesbian now? I don't know who would knock that up!! Maybe it was one of those Good Charlotte guys. Isn't it so weird, it's like, 8 years ago they sang about how rich and famous people suck, and now they're rich and famous themselves!!! OMG, it's like, so crazy!!! They should totally have to give the profits from that song to charity now!!! WTF, bro!! ROTFL!!!

Anyway, where was I? Hmm, I can't remember. Oh well, I'm sure it was nothing important.

9
Aliens suck

On July 8, 2011, scientists across the globe shed a tear when NASA launched its final shuttle into space. A victim of budget cuts and a failing economy, NASA saw its space shuttle program shut down — at least temporarily — by President Obama and Congress. A lot of people were very upset by this.

I am not one of those people.

Outer space sucks. It's nothing but blackness, flying rocks, and flashing lights. If you want to see that, you... well I'll spare you all a Source Awards joke and let's just move forward.

You see, when it comes to the space program, we're all lying to ourselves. Everywhere you turn, there's someone championing the benefits of space exploration. They say that we can study the surface of Mars and use the lessons that we learn to help us here on Earth. They say that studying the properties of distant atmospheres can lead to amazing breakthroughs in the fields like engineering and healthcare. They tell us that the space program leads to all sorts of side-projects, like Tang and cool bubble-dome helmets.

The truth is that we don't care about any of that. All we care about is discovering alien life. It's a fantasy for millions of Americans and it's every NASA employee's wet dream. We can make excuses about science, exploration, and the American Dream. At the end of the day, all we want is to meet an alien.

Not me, though.

Everyone thinks that discovering aliens is going to be so awesome. I blame Hollywood. We've seen so many movies like *E.T.* and *Independence Day*, we assume aliens are either hyper-intelligent beings who will guide us in our quest to advance our own society, or war-mongering mutants who will force an interstellar war for domination of the galaxy. We think aliens will show us amazing new technology or use amazing new technology to blow us up. Either way, we love it.

I don't doubt that there could be life on other planets. I'm not saying it's definite, but it's highly possible. Given the vastness of the universe, the finite number of atom combinations, and the unoriginality with which rocks crash into each other, it's very likely that somewhere out there, other planets have atmospheres that can sustain life. If aquatic conditions can exist on Jupiter's moon, imagine what's possible when you look further than three planets away.

Aliens could definitely exist.

However, I think we have seriously underestimated the odds of those aliens sucking. We search for life on other planets, but we never even consider the possibility that maybe we don't want to meet what's out there. Aliens could be annoying. They could be dicks that try to attack us. They could see Earthlings, and believe that we're the evil aliens, and attack us in self-defense.

Worst of all, they could be boring. There's a very good chance that aliens aren't as advanced as humans. TV shows and movies always portray aliens as geniuses. What if they're primitive creatures that can't even communicate? We'd essentially be traveling 50,000 light years to find a groundhog. Even if aliens are brilliant, they're not going to speak English. Communicating with aliens is going to be like talking to a coyote or a tennis ball. Best-case scenario, they'll communicate through a series of clicks, like those African tribes. Then we'll have to take 30 more years to fly an African click language translator over to galaxy XQ78, star 3B, planet 14. Where are we going to get the money for that? African click language translators are notorious for demanding first-class space flight amenities, and I already pay enough taxes.

What if aliens have a method of communication that we could never possibly understand? Maybe in alien culture, blinking seven times in rapid succession means "go to the bathroom before we head over to Uncle Steve's house" and waving hello and reaching for a handshake is their international sign for "I come to destroy your culture, you worthless fucks." We'll be knee-deep in intergalactic battle before we figure out what happened. I don't know why we expect to walk right up to aliens and immediately engage in meaningful conversation.

What if we find alien life, but don't realize it? We forget this, but plants are living things. If an alien came to Earth and saw a tree, he wouldn't try talking to it. He'd assume it was a tall rock. "Why are there green things hanging off this big rock?" That's what he'd say, in his alien click language. Couldn't aliens be like plants? What if aliens are blobs of gel, slithering around at .01 MPH?

What if aliens are the exact same as clock radios, only they have a spleen instead of an AM/FM switch? I'm telling you, it's gonna suck when we cross the entire galaxy and spend $90 trillion to find a clock radio with a spleen that performs photosynthesis.

Let's assume we find aliens one day. The odds of there being unfathomable and unbreakable communication barriers between us and them, thus rendering our discovery worthless, is 92%. The odds of an intergalactic war are 7%. The odds of them being really cool and telling us how to fix Earth's problems is 0.00000001%. The remaining odds say they'll be pretty decent, but have a few annoying quirks, like telling the same stories over and over and never getting to the stuff about laser beam technology.

Why put so much effort into something when there's so little chance of a payout? Scientists are going to tell you that we can study and learn from alien life, regardless of what that life is. Don't believe the hype. We've studied dolphins for like 30 years, and what have we learned? Nothing. Oh sure, we figured out that they communicate through sonar or sonic booms or some shit like that, but nothing we've learned is applicable to my life in any way. It's like my grandfather used to say, "Ain't no dolphin gonna pay my electric bill." My grandfather was an illiterate man, but his message was clear. We're spending millions of dollars on our space program when the average American is being crushed by debt and fisted by taxes. And for what? To discover aliens who are inevitably going to suck? Screw that. Aliens are assholes. Oh, you might meet an alien, but then you give them your phone number and they NEVER call.

10
Justin Bieber Sucks

Right now, in the music world, there's nobody bigger than Justin Bieber.

Justin Bieber sucks.

For starters, he only appeals to 14-year old girls. 14-year old girls are idiots, so therefore, via the transitive theory, Justin Bieber is worthless. His songs are derivative and cheesy. He sings like his balls are in a vice grip and his hair looks like something you'd see on sale for $9.99 at a Halloween store with the label "Men's Retro '60s Wig." The only good thing about "The Bieb" is that we'll eventually get to see him as a fat, washed-up 38-year-old with blond frosted tips, playing a murder suspect on "CSI: Saskatchewan" and trying to hawk his new album of Jesus songs.

Unfortunately Justin Bieber is only the tip of the shitty music iceberg. Have you heard pop music lately? What a pile of dog shit that is. The Black Eyed Peas sound like they stole their lyrics from a third grader's pop-up book, making Fergie's *Clumsy* video incredibly appropriate. Techno sounds like the musical equivalent of having someone drill into your cranium and then pour rubbing alcohol through the hole. Britney Spears is trailer trash, Lady Gaga dresses weird, and Christina Aguilera used to sleep with lots of guys so she's obviously awful. Pop music has always been terrible. Madonna was a little progressive but time passed and she aged and didn't die young or disappear so now you're an idiot if you ever thought she was good in the first place.

Rock music isn't much better. Indie bands are a bunch of pretentious pussies. They write a song about their iPod car adapter and it's supposed to symbolize the war on terror. Is that right? Because to me the only thing it symbolizes is your constant struggle to come to grips with a post-modern war-torn world in which your band sucks dick. And remember not so long ago when emo music was popular? Christ almighty. All emo bands are shit. The only good thing about being an emo fan is that you'll eventually cut your wrists too deep and die, thus sparing yourself from having to listen to emo music. Unless of course there's emo in heaven, but then again, wouldn't that make it hell? Oh, and let's not forget about Nickelback and the 80,000 Nickelback clones growling about bar fights and pussy and other stupid shit. If I paid 5 cents to hear Chad Kroeger sing, I'd ask for my nickel back and then stab whoever tricked me into that terrible deal in the first place. Every band whose singer has a deep voice is terrible. These bands like Creed and Theory of a Deadman sound like terrible Pearl Jam rip-offs. Eddie Vedder was a shitty version of Jim Morrison, so that should tell you how awful Scott Stapp is. It's funny that Scott Stapp always does Jesus poses, because even God hates Creed. It's in the Bible, look it up.

What about rap? All rap music is garbage. It's just a bunch of thugs talking about guns and cars and necklaces. They have nothing to say. Older rappers like Tupac and Biggie used to have something to say. Of course they were thugs who killed each other, so they suck too. Rap makes society dumber and it's destroying music. Anyone who listens to rap has an IQ of 40 and will shoot your children.

Music hasn't been relevant since 1969. U2 sucks and Bono is an asshole. Tom Petty, John Mellencamp, and Bruce Springsteen are populist douchebags who sing anthems for retarded frat guys and stupid sorority girls. Led Zeppelin and the Rolling Stones stole all their ideas from black people. The Beatles are the only halfway decent band that ever existed, but they once covered a Chuck Berry song, and Michael J. Fox played that one Chuck Berry song in *Back To The Future*, and the plot of that movie was absolutely ridiculous, and Ringo Starr was an average drummer at best, so the Beatles suck.

The only good music came way before the Beatles. Blues musicians were OK but most of them spent all their time telling stories about selling their souls to the devil or drowning in the Mississippi River rather than focusing on the craft. Robert Johnson was all hype. There were old folk musicians, but they all sang about the same topics. 1800s folk musicians had no range. And of course you had the farmers who used to whistle while they ploughed their fields. Those guys were OK when they first came out, but their later whistling was derivative and became a bad caricature of their early work. They never grew as artists. Before that, you had Native Americans and their rain dances. From a music theory standpoint they were alright, but they were really just doing it to help grow crops. Fuckin' sellouts. Music is an art form, not a method for growing squash, cockbags! And don't get me started on the ancient Europeans and their "Greensleeves" style ballads. Those jackasses were only in it for the pussy.

The only credible musician in history is Steven Wallace IV, who lived in Northern Ireland in the 8th Century. He was fleeing the British Army when he stopped and started scraping a stick against a tree. It was a hollow twig, and he was scraping a well-aged oak tree, so the acoustics were phenomenal. The rest of his Northern Irish brethren kept telling him, "Knock off that racket, the Brits are on their way!" But Wallace kept scraping the stick against the tree, claiming, "I don't care about the Brits, I like the way this sounds." Now that guy was in it for the right reasons. He didn't care about the public reaction or the money or even his life, he was all about the art, man. He continued practicing his craft even as his group left him. Eventually he was captured and beheaded by the British Army. What a tragedy. That guy had so much more greatness in him.

That guy who scraped a stick against a tree in the 8th Century was the only true musician to ever live. Everyone since him has sucked. Especially Justin Bieber.

11
The Best Things in Life Are Really Expensive

I was reading an article on MSN.com earlier titled "Will Our Kids Be Dumb & Broke?," and it really made me think about… umm… something, I guess. I don't know, I was too busy sending my bank account info to this chick Natasha. She's from Russia. We met on Craigslist. She's totally hot for me, but she can't afford a plane ticket to America. So she asked if I could loan her $2,000. I know, I know, it's a lot of money, but the minute her plane lands in New York I'm sure it'll seem like a small price to pay for discovering true love. Anyway, I didn't completely grasp the idea of this article, but I think it was something about how young people make unwise decisions with money.

This is a topic that most people can relate to. Older people always talk about how they wish they made smarter decisions when they were younger. Most of the time this is just old people being jealous of young people and trying to trick us into acting "responsible." Responsibility is a code word for "lame," and that's why it's best to ignore the advice of your elders at all times. Once in awhile, though, adults are right about stuff. And one piece of advice that most adults agree upon is that you need to save money starting right after college. If you wait until your 30s or later to start saving, you've already missed out on your greatest chance to build wealth.

The problem with this concept, of course, is that stuff is expensive. Everything costs money. Think about it: You can barely leave the house without paying. It costs money to drive anywhere. You can't go to bars or restaurants without running up a solid tab. Movies are expensive, as is a cable bill. There is nothing free you can do for fun, at least nothing worth doing. Even when something is free, like say going to a public beach, they'll hit you up for parking or find another way to get money out of you. Oh sure, technically there are free activities, like going for a walk, but if walking was so great then why did God invent cars? Yeah, exactly.

They say you should budget 50% of your income for fixed bills — rent, car payments, insurance, student loans, etc. — and save the rest for leisure, food, and emergencies. For most young people, especially those of us who live in urban areas, that's simply not realistic. Rent and the costs of owning a car are especially high these days, so even on a decent income, after they've paid fixed bills, many people have far less than half of their paycheck left over. Finding money to save means cutting into your disposable income. In other words, it cuts into your fun.

I have this crazy theory. I don't think fun should be treated as a bonus, reserved for times when you have a surplus of disposable income. Fun is a necessary cost of living. I believe spending money on fun is as important — if not more — than things like rent and car payments. Now, you can't be stupid about it. You need a place to live, and you have to buy food. But if I had a choice between a great apartment and a boring social life, or an average apartment and a great social life, I'll take the latter every time. When it comes down to saving for retirement in your 20s versus being able to go out and have fun whenever you want, I think you have to go with fun.

Sure, you could cost yourself hundreds of thousands of potential dollars in your 401K by not saving right out of college, but if you're sitting at home all day so that you can save for the future, what's the point? You're costing yourself life, dammit! Sorry, I couldn't think of a way to make that not sound cheesy. Seriously though, how do you know there won't be another financial scandal that leaves you broke? How do you know you won't get mauled by a bear? How do you know you won't get a huge promotion or marry some rich geriatric or win the lottery and be set for life, thus rendering all time spent saving worthless? No one has ever looked back on their life and said, "Man, I wish I never had all those awesome times when I was young!"

Recently, I spent several hundred dollars to get wasted all day and see Stone Temple Pilots on their reunion tour. I didn't need to spend that much. I didn't have to get VIP seats. I didn't have to get a hotel room and stay over after the show. But I did. Those few hundred dollars could've gone toward retirement, but then I wouldn't have seen Scott Weiland wearing a poncho, yelling into a megaphone and doing the Scott Weiland Dance. A lot of people would call my spending frivolous, and say that in the long run, I'd be better off cutting back on my leisure expenses and putting more money toward my future. To which I would respond, "Have you heard 'Crackerman?'"

Some of my fondest memories are nights spent out in New York City with my friends. When I lived in Manhattan, friends would visit me constantly, and showing them a good time in the city nearly bankrupt me. After I moved north to Connecticut, the cost of taking public transportation and going out to bars with my NYC friends was absurd. Spending money was way too easy. I'd go down to the city with $200 in my wallet and still find myself at the ATM before the night was over. Every Saturday night I didn't go out drinking was an extra $100 I could spend on bills, groceries, gas, video games, or thousands of other tangible goods.

That was in my twenties. Now I'm 30 years old. And guess what? I would pay twice as much to do it all over again. All my friends have gone down separate paths over the past few years. Most are in serious relationships. Many are married and several have kids. The only thing that can get everyone together is a major (and expensive) event, like a wedding. Nowadays we end up spending twice the money to have half as much fun as we used to. I'm not trying to depress anyone with this information. Being thirty isn't that bad. Things change and you develop different priorities, so going out and partying doesn't seem so important any more. But I'll always look back fondly on my twenties, since those years were undoubtedly the most fun I'll ever have. If I had followed the advice of investment professionals or "wealth specialists," I'd have a little more money right now, but my life wouldn't be nearly as rich.

Those who can afford to save money and still live it up are fortunate. If you can only afford one of the two, I don't think it's wise to pass on enjoying your twenties just so you can be financially secure when you're 70. You can always work to increase your savings later in life. You can never replace missed experiences.

By the way, when I'm fifty and have a retirement fund worth $300, and you find me face down in a ditch with a bottle of Colt 45 screaming "Why, WHYYY?!?!," ask me if I'll reconsider my position. Then get out of the way before I stab you.

12
Solving the World's Problems with Rap Lyrics: High Gas Prices

In this world of ours, there is no shortage of difficult issues. From poverty to war to an unfair class structure, there are too many troubling problems facing society today. And sadly, many young people just don't care. Sure, some pretend to be interested in the issues, but when it comes time to take action, they turn their backs on the important topics at hand.

Fortunately, there is a way to reach the youth of the world. Yes, one method of communication has proven highly effective when it comes to reaching out and inspiring young people the world over.

And that, my friends, is rap music.

Young people are the future, and if we're going to improve this planet of ours then we need the youth to be involved. In an effort to inspire, motivate, and solve all of the world's most troubling issues, I have decided to get young people involved the only way I know how: By creating hot new rap lyrics.

Right now I'd like to tackle one of the world's most pressing current issues...

High gas prices.

Hopefully the following rap song I wrote will give kids a new perspective and solve this issue once and for all.

****

"F**k Gas Prices (F**k 'em Real Good)"
by Yung Teezy

Every day I wake up and go ridin' in my Hummer
I pass the gas station, can't believe them fuckin' numbers
$3.85, four dollas, $4.50 shawty
That's a whole lotta money that I can't spend on Bacardi
What's a playa s'posed to do? How's a real thug s'posed to shoot?
When an AK-47 cost less than the commute
To the gun store, where the prices always getting higher
You see them gas prices, they's affectin' the suppliers
To keep those trucks on the road, I'm paying extra tax on groceries
You expect me to cut back on Cristal, naw that ain't cool B
So I stopped buying Magnums just to save a little income
Now I got 7 new mouths to feed, aww shit, son

Man fuck them gas prices
(Yeah fuck them real good!)
Man, fuck them gas prices
(Yeah fuck them real good!)
Man, fuck gas prices
Yeah fuck 'em!!

So I complained and complained, but then I realized
Gotta shut my diamond-encrusted mouth and open my eyes

Gotta walk more, carpool, find a better way
Gotta consume less petroleum and way more Alizé
Gotta drive less, ride a bike, go out for less dinners
Gotta buy a Hybrid Escalade with some fly-ass spinners
Let's improve our global standing, let's stop acting like snitches
Let's break our dependence on foreign oil and depend on foreign bitches
If we don't make some changes, our economy gon' be dead
I'm-a save myself some cash by fucking ho's on a moped
And with all these extra dollas in my pocket that keep forming
I'm-a make it rain, gonna stop global warming
We all gotta make changes, let's all reach for the stars
Don't want my 42 kids growin' up in a world without cars
Let's reject this agenda Exxon Mobil be sellin'
Let's keep on ballin' while we keep on yellin'…

Man fuck them gas prices
(Yeah fuck them real good!)
Man, fuck them gas prices
(Yeah fuck them real good!)
Man, fuck gas prices
Yeah fuck 'em!!

Uhh, yeah, man, $4.08, $3.95, uhh, $4.12 up in this piece, shout out to my man corn oil, yeah, yeah, fuck them gas prices, uhh, all night long baby

13
The Meaning of Life, Part II

In 1963, Bob Dylan released the song "Blowin' in the Wind," an acoustic ballad that poses myriad existential questions about life, freedom, and basic human rights. The refrain of the song states quite simply that the answer to these questions "is blowin' in the wind."

Dylan's ability to blend rich metaphors with a captivating narrative is one of the main reasons his song have remained popular for decades.

However, I've always thought it would be great if someone referenced this song while asking me a deep existential question, but instead of it being a metaphor, it turned out the answer was literally blowing in the wind next to me. Like someone would say, "What's the meaning of life? The answer my friend is blowing in the wind." And then a piece of paper would fly into my hand and I'd open it and go, "Children. It's children."

14
Question For God

If you had the chance to meet God and ask him just one question, what would it be?

I'm sure a lot of you are thinking of the standard questions, like "why are we here?" and "what's the secret to eternal happiness?" A few of you are even thinking, "how can I be really, really rich?" You damn Jews.

Well, if I had the opportunity to ask just one question to God, it would be this:

"Why do bees sting?"

Does that sound like a crazy question to ask? Yes. But is it stupid? Absolutely not. Because this question could change the way that everyone in the entire world views everything.

How? First let's backtrack a little…

One of the expressions that you'll hear all the time is "Everything happens for a reason." This is mostly a Christian thing, but not exclusively; people of every race, religion, and creed, including the members of the band Creed, have been known to utter this phrase. It *is* almost always used as a justification for the bad things that happen in life. Think about how many times something awful has happened to someone, followed by someone else uttering the phrase, "well, everything happens for a reason." As if that drunk driver who totaled your car was a little package from heaven sent to help you in the long run. Oftentimes this phrase will be used when the tragic event is already long past. For example, someone who is laid off might find a better job three months later, and then claim that they were originally laid off because "everything happens for a reason."

Here's the problem: Bad stuff happens to everyone, and good things happen to everyone as well. These things happen at random times, with no particular rhyme or reason. So whenever something really bad happens to you, unless you end up dying, you will eventually have something else happen afterwards that is good. It's not destiny. It's the way it is. If you get mugged and beat down and robbed, then two weeks later you win the lottery, it is not divine will. It's your dumb ass walking down a dark alley at night, and your blind luck picking a winning lottery ticket. Two completely unrelated events. Although they both relate to a loss and gain of money, they are not tied in any way.

Now, I've been a firm believer in karma ever since Radiohead's *OK Computer* album came out in 1997 and featured the single "Karma Police." Karma is not the same as "everything happens for a reason." Karma is the belief that if you do the right things and live life in a positive way, you will eventually be rewarded. The reason karma works is because a positive person who does the right things will appear more attractive to the opposite sex, be promoted at work, and generally be held in the highest esteem by others. This leads to opportunities that the angry and pessimistic guy down the block doesn't have. You bring this good "luck" upon yourself with your actions and demeanor.

The "everything happens for a reason" idea is the exact opposite. This is for the lazy man; the man who loses his job and then says, "Hey, everything happens for a reason" and does nothing about it. Yeah, it happened for a reason... cause you sucked at your job. Now put down the Marlboro Reds, turn off WWE Friday Night Smackdown, and go find a new job, and this time don't fall asleep while you're driving the forklift.

When you lose a job, it's not random luck. It's usually the economy or incompetence. When you get into a car accident, it's not random luck. It's because some asshole ran a red light while text-messaging his girlfriend. When you break up with someone and then meet someone better down the road, it's not random luck. It's because you were terrible in bed but finally found out about the wonderful benefits of natural male enhancement thanks to an e-mail with some exceptionally convincing copywriting that snuck through your computer's spam filter. By using the "everything happens for a reason" logic, you are essentially denying responsibility for whatever happens to you, rather than admitting that something *may* have been your fault.

Don't get me wrong, denying responsibility can be great. Like if your dog shits on the neighbor's lawn, and the neighbor wants you to clean it up, you would want to deny that. "Sorry Steve, I don't know what you're talking about, I don't even own a dog," you would say while kicking your puppy in the ribcage so it stopped barking. That's not why I hate the phrase. No, why I dislike the phrase "everything happens for a reason" is because it has become the go-to excuse for religious people. This is what religious people say anytime something awful happens. They think, "certainly MY God would never send a massive hurricane that wiped out most of the Gulf Coast. After all, my God is great." So when their God does send a massive hurricane that wipes out most of the Gulf coast, including the home of Mardi Gras and the New Orleans Saints football team, they are left with no explanation. So they say "everything happens for a reason," and they go back about their business.

Listen, I have no idea if God exists. Maybe he's exactly like they say in the Bible, or maybe he doesn't exist at all. Maybe it's somewhere in-between. I have no clue. You put aside the issue of faith and stick to straight facts, and the truth is that nobody truly knows what the deal is with this "God" character.

But I do know this: If we are to believe there is a God, and that He created mankind, and that He is somehow responsible for everything that happens in our lives... well then we should definitely hold him accountable for his work.

I'm all for praising God for the wonders of life. A beautiful sunset? Nice work, God. The sights of this great country, like the Grand Canyon and Niagara Falls? Tremendous, way to go G-man. Megan Fox's ass? Fantastic fucking work. But if we're going to praise the good, shouldn't we also question God for all the shitty stuff in this world? Poverty? No good, God. Hate and oppression? Not so hot, father man. AIDS in Africa? Dude, you really boned that one.

It should be a give-and-take relationship. You can't just praise God for the glory of life while glossing over all the bad stuff. Somehow God is up there in heaven, cruising around in his Hummer H2 with Marilyn Monroe and Elvis, getting a free ride from everyone down here. Job accountability... That's what it's all about, people. If you blow your big account at work, can you just go into your bosses office and tell him "hey, don't worry about it, everything happens for a reason?" You can, but then he'll say, "Yes, that's an excellent point, now pack up your shit and get out."

Before you get your panties in a bunch, know that this is not meant to be a criticism of God. I don't know about you, but I would prefer a God with some faults. The current God is supposedly flawless. He can do no wrong. He's infallible. He's like that one dude at every school who gets the hottest chick, has the perfect body, is captain of the football team, has a 4.0 GPA, is loved by all teachers and parents, and saves kittens from burning buildings in his spare time. Let's be honest, we all hate that dude. He's dating the cheerleader and he's responsible for the miracle of life, but meanwhile he's also kind of stuck-up and he might have caused that tsunami in Indonesia. God might be the Class President, but he won't even let you sit at his lunch table.

On the other hand, a not-so-perfect God, a God who makes mistakes, but a God who's doing the best he can with this shitty world... now that's my kind of God. My kind of God can't solve the poverty problem, because it's too damn big, so every once in awhile he lets some random Pakistani deli owner hit the lotto. You know, just so he's doing SOMETHING about it. My kind of God realizes that greed and corruption are out of control in the business world, so he develops a system where money and power don't correlate to true happiness. My kind of God can't stop hate and terrorism, but he at least makes terrorists live in a shitty ass desert without TV. My kind of God knows that everything doesn't happen for a reason, and that gives him a reason to make things happen.

Which brings us back to my one question to God.

"Why do bees sting?"

Why would this be my one question? Because this would prove beyond a shadow of a doubt that everything DOES NOT happen for a reason. There is absolutely no reason why bees should sting. Not one. Think about it for a second. Why DO bees sting people? There's no benefit to the people. A bee sting hurts. But it doesn't hurt too bad. It's not a life-altering, enlightening sort of pain, like a car crash victim might experience. It's more annoying than anything. It doesn't toughen you up and it doesn't improve your defense mechanisms whatsoever. You're still just as likely to be stung, and it's still just as annoying each time. There are no real ramifications to a bee sting other than mild annoyance. There's no lesson to be learned, and nothing about a bee sting will help you down the road. I mean, what do we learn from a bee sting? Don't stand around bees? Yeah, we already knew that. And what about the bees? Well, after a bee stings you, guess what? The bee dies. Yep, it loses its stinger and dies minutes later. So unless every bee on earth is actively trying to commit suicide, there is no purpose for the bee sting.

"Why *do* bees sting?"

How could God possibly answer this question? He can't. There is no answer. If I were to ask this, God would just end up standing there speechless, like the one overwhelmed kid who always gets further than he should at the Spelling Bee Championships and then freezes up when he has to spell "onomatopoeia." He'd stammer and ask me to use the phrase in a sentence before eventually admitting he didn't know, as all the smart Asian children in heaven looked on and laughed smugly to themselves.

And then we'd all know the truth…

Not EVERYTHING happens for a reason.

So, next time your best friend loses his job, watches his family die in a house fire, and discovers that he has leukemia all on the same day, then tries to justify it by saying that "everything happens for a reason"… You look him right in the eye, scoff condescendingly, and respond, "well, not EVERYTHING."

15
Rat-Flavored Hot Dogs Are a Metaphor For Life

If you've ever been to New York City, you're probably familiar with the street vendors that sell hot dogs.

If not, there are two things you need to know about these hot dogs:

1) They're delicious.

2) They're most likely made of rat.

One might think that rat meat in the form of a hot dog would be disgusting, but to the contrary, few culinary experiences match the ecstasy that is the rat dog.

The appeal is simple. No one ever buys a rat dog because they were in the mood. It's what you eat when you're starving, you're pressed for time, and you just happen to pass a vendor. Say you have to catch a train, and there's no time for dinner. Or maybe you got out of work incredibly late and you don't feel like cooking. That's when you pass a vendor on the street and decide to take the plunge into rat dog ecstasy. No one ever seeks out the rat dog. It's what you eat when you have no other option. But when you need it, the rat dog is always there, beckoning to the hungry like a beautiful Siren singing its sweet, sweet song. Thus it becomes a tremendous experience, like a lifeboat appearing to rescue you from the harsh sea of hunger.

Yet, there's a problem. Although the rat dog is absolutely delicious going down, it makes you feel like death shortly afterwards. Once you eat a rat dog, you have about a 30-minute window before your insides start to reject the rat meat and your stomach starts turning itself inside out to spew the vile hazard from your system. Don't get me wrong, it's a glorious 30 minutes, but you feel like crap for the rest of the day.

So knowing the dire after-effects of the rat dog, people are apt to avoid it, right?

Of course not. People devour rat dogs. Rat dogs are consumed in mass quantities on a daily basis. Don't think it's only naïve tourists eating these rat dogs. Oh no. Veteran New Yorkers love them as well. They willingly accept the death-like feeling just to have those fleeting minutes of joy that come during the rat dog consumption process.

This is why the rat dog is a metaphor for life. We all know the rat dog is terrible for you. We all know that, when you consume a rat dog, the feeling of death is inevitable. And yet, so many of us eat the rat dog on a regular basis anyway. The rat dog represents the choice of smart planning versus instant gratification.

Everyone wants to make the smart decision. We want to do what's best for ourselves in the long run. We want to save for retirement, develop an exercise plan, go to church on Sundays, work with a charity and become a better person. But when it comes down to it, what do we do? We blow all our money on things we don't need, we eat a bunch of ice cream, we get drunk on Saturday nights and sleep in late, we watch reality TV and we stay the exact same person we always have been. Why? Because it's easier. It's quicker. It offers an immediate result. The long-term plan might be smarter overall, but it doesn't help us *right now*.

So what are we supposed to do? Do we choose instant gratification, or the more rewarding long-term plan? What will you do next time you're put in a difficult predicament? Will you take the easy way out, or will you sacrifice short-term pleasures for a better and more meaningful existence? Will you eat the rat and ravage your stomach, or will you go hungry and save your soul?

I think I speak for all Americans when I say: I really want a fucking hot dog right now.

[*Note:* Most of the NYC street vendors also sell rat-flavored chicken strips. Those are somewhat better for you. You can get those instead of the hot dog, if you're a pussy.]

16
Everything I Know, I Learned on the Street

I always tell people that I've learned more on the street than I've ever learned in a classroom. Everyone assumes that I'm joking, that I'm trying to be funny by insinuating my upbringing was more akin to that of an impoverished and troubled youth from the ghetto than to the stereotypical life of someone in a lilywhite suburb like the one from whence I came.

But here's what people don't understand: I'm not joking. That's because when I say I learned more on the street than in the classroom, I mean that sentence absolutely literally.

The other day, I was walking down the street when I saw a few Snapple caps lying on the edge of the road. I picked them up, and much to my surprise, the underside of those caps taught me interesting tidbits such as the amount of time a human sleeps in an average lifetime or how many times a hummingbird can flap its wings in a minute. I guess Snapple has done this for a while now, but I'm not much of a Snapple drinker so I thought that shit was crazy. None of my teachers ever taught me how fast a hummingbird can flap its wings.

See what I mean? I have learned more while *literally on a street* than I've learned at school. To be fair, I'm including roads, alleys, byways, turnpikes and most other paved surfaces under my umbrella definition of "street." I've learned a thing or two on an avenue, and I've had my mind blown on a parkway. Hell, I've even learned stuff in parking lots.

One time I was walking down a street and a cool-looking car flew right by me. I was with a friend who likes cars, and he told me it was the new Maserati. I never knew what the new Maserati looked like, because that's the kind of thing you don't learn in school. I also learned that the Maserati's acceleration is phenomenal, when the driver had to stop at a stop sign a block later. I also realized Maserati drivers are dicks when the guy drove into a puddle and got water all over my khakis. You get the idea though. I didn't even know there was a new Maserati, because my teachers spent months dissecting the Battle of Gettysburg and never once taught me a thing about cars. I drive a car every single day, I've spent thousands of dollars on car maintenance, and most of the people I see on the highway don't know what the fuck they're doing, yet no school ever gives a class on the basics of car ownership. What the hell?

Another time I was taking a piss in this empty street behind a bar, and I accidentally stepped on a used condom. It was gross. That's when I learned the value of holding it and waiting in line. I never thought it was important to use actual bathrooms because health education in the public school systems focuses on unimportant stuff like the circulatory system. And since schools shy away from sex ed., I had no idea people liked to fuck in alleys behind bars. But hey, at least I knew how to properly clean a sneaker, right? Guess again, my friends. Once again I had to learn that on the street… my street… where my mom threw my disgusting sneakers after I wore them in the house.

My teacher always used to say that drunk driving ruins lives. But recently I drove by a billboard on the highway that said you don't have to suffer just because you've been arrested for drunk driving. I didn't know that before. And it had a picture of a shady-looking lawyer along with his e-mail and phone number, so I learned his contact info as well. Also, I was pretty wasted at the time, so I learned that sometimes you can drive drunk with no consequences whatsoever. WHY DID YOU LIE TO ME, MRS. BROWN?!?!?!

I learned teamwork while playing basketball on cement courts. I learned discipline while running ten miles in the rain through the roads of my hometown. I learned about racial harmony while playing a dice game with a bunch of black and Latino kids in someone's driveway. I learned about class differences when those same black and Latino kids won all my money and then asked me to give them a ride to the dollar store so they could use it to purchase food for their family, which I happily did on my way to buy $100 ripped jeans at Abercrombie. I even learned the secret to eternal happiness while standing on a sidewalk. That one was pure coincidence. I happened to meet a really insightful guy at last year's St. Patrick's Day parade.

I learned all of that stuff in one place. It's the same place I learned common sense, or how to interact with others, or how to act in the presence of an authority figure, or how to compose an e-mail or treat a woman or do any of the other things that play a drastic role in my everyday life. I didn't learn them in school, that's for sure. I learned them in a street. *The* street.

So when I say that I learned more on the street than I did in the classroom, you better believe I'm telling the truth.

Of course, I've learned more from TV than I did from either of those two stupid places.

17
Not a Pirate

You're not a pirate if you don't wear an eyepatch. You're not a pirate without a parrot, or at least some sort of exotic bird on your shoulder. And you're certainly not a pirate if you carry an AK-47. If you're just some 16-year old Somalian kid with a semi-automatic handgun, that makes you a thug. Not a pirate.

In April of 2009, a group of young Somalian "pirates" took over a U.S. ship, resulting in an infamous standoff and the eventual killing of 3 Somalians by U.S. Naval sharpshooters. Pirating has always been a problem in that region of the world, but this one incident brought massive media attention, and ever since we've learned about a rash of pirate attacks on both Americans and citizens of other nations. It's been tragic to watch. The loss of lives is bad enough, but the laziness with which these pirates go about their craft is downright appalling. I know some people like to think that hijacking boats automatically qualifies you as a pirate, but I'm sorry, that's simply not the case. I hate to sound old-fashioned, but I remember when being a pirate used to mean something. It was about having a merry old time with a bunch of oddly dressed pirate cohorts, singing drunken songs about the sea until an ocean liner came along and gave you the chance to steal a pirate's booty and make a captain walk the plank. You used to engage in sword-to-sword duels over sunken treasure. You used to fight off scurvy in order to bang disgusting wenches and get syphilis. You used to care. You didn't just waltz up to a barge with an

AK-47 and shoot the joint up. That was the lazy man's way out. Real pirates used to take their job seriously.

Carrying an AK-47 in a motorboat doesn't make you a pirate. It makes you a car-jacker. A very wet car-jacker. Is that what you want to do with your life? Is this what you want to be? Huh?? IS IT??? Oh, you can call yourself a pirate all you want, but if you don't wield a sword in your hand and a parrot on your shoulder with a funny hat on your head, you're really nothing more than a thug in a crappy boat with an AK. Remember that.

There was a time when people used to go about their careers with passion, and strive for excellence at all times, regardless of their occupation. It didn't matter if you were the captain, the janitor, the mid-level pirate accountant, or the lowest wench on the totem pole. You tried. Now everyone looks for the easy way out, showing up late, checking out early, doing the bare minimum and brandishing an AK-47 for a job that requires the finesse of a curved sword and a silly hat. People used to take pride in their jobs. Now they don't. Not even the pirates. And you know what, it's sad. No wonder our economy is in shambles.

18

Trying to Calculate the Amount of Money I've Spent on Alcohol in My Life

I'm not the President of the United States. I'm not a Congressman, or a CEO, or even a middle manager. I don't own stock in a Fortune 500 Company. I don't own a home. I bought my car used. I rarely go out to dinner and I occasionally struggle to pay my bills.

Why?

Am I a loser? Do I underachieve? Was I dealt a bad hand in life? Am I the product of an unfair system? Have I slipped through the cracks? Am I a child left behind? Have I suffered the wrath of a harsh economy that systematically squeezes out the middle class?

No.

I drink.

I should note that I am in no way complaining about this. I happen to think drinking is awesome. I've enjoyed every night spent at the bar, and I regret nothing. Nevertheless, I'd like to show you, through simple economics, how drinking has prevented me from achieving all of my dreams.

This is my rough estimation of how much money I've spent on alcohol in my entire life.

High School

I drank only occasionally in high school. Instead I spent my time doing things like bowling, mini-golf, hanging out with friends, doing schoolwork, helping others... you know, the lame shit you do before you realize how great booze is. While attending high school parties, I almost exclusively drank Beast Light, which runs $4.88 for a 12-pack with tax and deposit. Yes, I remember the exact price. Of course, the local neighborhood market charged an "underage tax." It was an unspoken extra charge added on top of your purchase. If you questioned the price, they asked for your ID. We never questioned the price. When all was said and done, it ended up being closer to $10 for a 12-pack. During this time, my friends and I only went to house parties or parties in the woods. This was good and bad. Good in that there were never any cover charges, but bad in that we may have at one point started a forest fire. I actually can't comment about that. The important thing is we saved money. I also once stole three 24-packs from the country club where I worked. I'm not proud of this, but being in high school is like being in prison; you do whatever you have to do to survive. Given all of this information, I would estimate I only spent about $500 on alcohol throughout high school.

High School total = $500

College

Then came college. The heaviest drinking of my life was

done while at college. Like most people, I spent most of my collegiate career under the influence, partying 4-5 nights a week for the majority of my tenure. Freshmen and sophomore year, I had a budget of $60 per week, in addition to my meal plan, to spend on food and beverage. Once a week, I would throw in $5 to split a pizza with friends. The rest went toward alcohol. Whether it was a cover to a frat party or a bottle of Mr. Boston vodka that I snuck past security, booze was my lone expense. The meal plan covered all my food, and I was good about not eating out. I wore the same gray hooded sweatshirt and jeans every day, so I never bought any clothes. Any girlfriend-related expenses were kept to a minimum, which is probably the reason those relationships didn't work out.

Junior and senior year, I got a job as a substitute teacher. This, shockingly and unethically, did not cut into my drinking whatsoever. However, it did raise my alcohol budget to about $80 a week. In addition, it allowed me to finally purchase things like clothing and real food. Looking back, it's funny, but at the time, you never realize how broke you are, and how shitty your living conditions are while you're in college. Most people in Section 8 housing live a more luxurious life than I did at age 20.

With the amounts listed above, we're looking at $4,995 spent on drinking during my four years of college. Then you have to add the $200 that I spent on my two fake IDs, and the $500 that I spent to attend my Senior Booze Cruise and Senior Formal, which was nothing more than an excuse to drink in fancy clothes. Oh, and let's not forget the two spring break trips I took to Cancun and Key West. That's another $4,000, easy.

But wait. That doesn't count the 15 weeks a year I was on break from school. My drinking didn't stop when I took off my Marist College sweatshirt. I'm being metaphorical, of course. I wouldn't wear the shirt of the college I was attending. That's like wearing the shirt of the band you're going to see. Point is, I went home and drank with my high school friends. I did work during summer breaks, which gave me less time to party, so I'd estimate my alcohol budget during breaks was closer to $40/week. That's an additional $2,400 over four years. I'm going to go ahead and add an extra $300 as the amount I spent to buy my brother alcohol before he turned 21. Don't judge me. It was a different time, back in 2002.

College total = $12,295

Manhattan

After college, I moved to Manhattan. The nice thing about having a real job is, you finally have some money. The bad part is, you can't drink Natty Light at the Kappa Kappa Gamma house with 18-year olds any more. Well, you can, but it's not a good idea. I was forced to start drinking at classier establishments, and my wallet took a hit. If you've never been to Manhattan, it's fucking expensive. An average night out cost me around $80. That's with pre-gaming. It's insane. I went out every Friday and Saturday, and usually on Thursdays as well. Let's call it $200 a week. After a year of living in Manhattan, I was broke, exhausted, and most likely left with severe liver damage.

Manhattan = $10,400

Connecticut

In 2005, I moved north to Connecticut. I've lived here ever since, shuffling around between Stamford, Norwalk, and Hartford. You would think that this would have saved me money, but unfortunately, I'm an idiot, so for years I went back to New York City every third weekend to party with my New York friends. Even when I stay in The Nutmeg State, I've found that it isn't cheap to drink here. Turns out there's no such thing as a free liquid lunch. Connecticut bars all charge a cover, and I would never show up at a house party without a 30-rack of Busch Light. It just wouldn't be polite. I can easily spend $200 during a weekend of hard partying in Connecticut, but in the interest of fairness, let's just say my alcohol costs have been $500 a month since I've been living here. I've lived in Connecticut for six years now, but I've been curtailing my drinking over the past few years, so I'm only going to count fours of those years and call it a life. Four years at $500/month: That's almost worse than Connecticut taxes. Almost.

Connecticut = $24,000

Additional Expenses

The above totals represent only alcoholic beverages, tips, and cover charges. There are many, many other expenses that I could justify as drinking-related.

The first is rent. I've paid a lot of extra money in rent in order to live in downtown areas with bars and restaurants. I could have been living cheaply in the Connecticut suburbs for the past five years, but I refused to spend my twenties wallowing in the boredom of suburban life. I wanted to be close to the party. My rent was always at least $100/month higher because of that choice.

The amount of money I've spent to travel to friends' parties is incredible. I've lived in a few different locations, so I have friends throughout the Northeast. They range from Boston down to D.C., and everywhere in between. For years I traveled all over the place, going to different parties in order to see all my friends. I was gone so often, my friends in Connecticut used to joke that I was on a "Northeast Tour." It's impossible to determine the cost of all this traveling, what with gas, food, and the occasional hotel, but rest assured I've spent over $10,000 in my life just getting to parties.

The quantity of unnecessary late-night food I've eaten could feed a small African nation. And I can't begin to tell you all of the stupid shit I've purchased and the stupid bets I've made when I was drunk. Again, this is impossible to quantify, but just to give you an example, I once ordered an entire Oreo Cream Pie from Denny's at 2AM. A slice of Oreo Cream Pie runs about $4. A pie is six slices. When I ordered it, the waitress was astounded. I had to repeat myself and specify that I wanted the full Oreo pie, not just a slice. Apparently nobody has asked for the whole pie before. I ate half of it, and with the sugar rush, I couldn't fall sleep until 7AM that day. Now, extrapolate that kind of behavior over the course of ten years and you'll begin to see the unwise choices I make with money when alcohol is involved.

Finally, there are weddings. I know some people treat weddings as a cherished event, but for my friends, weddings are nothing more than an expensive excuse to get plastered. Hell, even if I don't like a friend's girlfriend or boyfriend, I'll still tell them to get married, just so I have another massive party to go to. I've been to roughly 25 weddings since I graduated college. On average, they cost me $350. That includes hotel, gift, and various travel expenses. I've also been to one destination wedding, in Key West. That one probably cost me $1,500. So right there, you're talking about almost $10,000 for what amounts to a series of glorified open bars.

Consider all these expenses, which are clearly a byproduct of drinking, and we're talking about roughly another $35,000 in alcohol-related costs.

THE DAMAGE

Without taking into account any of the additional expenses listed above, I've spent an estimated $47,195 on booze in my lifetime. That's alcohol, tips, and cover charges. I want to stress that I was cautious in my estimations. The actual cost is surely even higher.

The average median household income in the United States is $50,000. That's for two people, before taxes. If I never had a drink, I would be able to support a family of four for two years. I would have enough for down payments on two separate houses. I'd be able to buy a brand-new BMW, or two brand-new Honda Civics. I could pay for a year of college at an Ivy League school, or three years at a state school. I could start my own Internet company and probably keep it afloat for a couple of years.

That's how much I've spent on alcohol.

Throw in the additional expenses, and we're up to $85,000. Again, that's a very conservative estimate. Eighty-five thousand dollars is a half a house, a fleet of cars, or college for one of my future children. Think of where I'd be with an extra $85,000. With smart investing, I could potentially make millions, or at least assure myself of a healthy retirement.

And that's what alcohol has cost me.

The big question is, do I regret it? Hell no. I accumulated a lifetime's worth of memories before the age of thirty, so in my mind, it was worth every penny. In fact, before I started these calculations, I was expecting the total to be higher, maybe somewhere in the region of $100,000. I may not own a house, or a new car, or my own company, or shares of Google stock, but $85,000 for a decade of fun seems like a fair deal.

Just don't tell my girlfriend she could be dating a rich guy. She'll fucking kill me.

19
The Holiday Calendar According to Tom Z

Anyone who knows me knows that I'm the All-American guy. I love hot dogs, apple pie, Ultimate Fighting, imperialism, The Cheesecake Factory, and all of the other things that make America the greatest country in the world.

There is one thing I don't like about America, however: The holidays. Oh, don't get me wrong, I love Fourth of July and Thanksgiving as much as the rest of you, but I feel like our holiday schedule as a whole needs to be streamlined. For starters, why do we have all these holidays that no one gets off from work? Oh, I know, it's an "observance," not a holiday. I say, if you have to work, it's not a holiday or an observance, it's a workday. Arbor Day? More like... well, nothing rhymes with "arbor," but the point is that holiday blows. Therefore I've done everyone the favor of creating a new holiday calendar, one that peels back the layers of nonsense and delivers a crisp, 16-day holiday schedule for all Americans to abide by. Each of the dates below would be a federally-mandated holiday, and NO ONE would ever have to go to work on any of these days. Because, after all, the important thing about a holiday isn't celebrating freedom, practicing religious traditions, or honoring historical figures... it's staying home from work.

Without further ado, I present:

The Holiday Calendar According to Tom Z

December 31 – January 1st – New Year's Eve / New Year's Day

Under my new calendar, New Year's Day would remain untouched. New Year's Eve, however, would become an official holiday where no one was forced to work. After all, you've got more important things to do on December 31st, like buying handles of vodka and noisemakers.

January - Third Monday – Great Historical Figures Day

Winter holidays. There's Martin Luther King Day. Washington's Birthday. Lincoln's Birthday. President's Day. Billy Fuccillo's Holiday Hyundai Selldown Event. It sounds great, having a bunch of different holidays to honor individual historical legends. But in reality, it only dilutes the quality of each historical figure's day. Some companies give you Martin Luther King Day off, some give you President's Day off, some give both and some give neither. Sometimes kids get a week off school and sometimes they get one Monday. You can't plan a vacation during this time because you never know which of the days you have off. It's chaos. Plus, isn't it kind of dumb to honor great figures in history by letting kids stay home from school and skip history class 3 different times every winter? That's why, like Billy Fuccillo, I believe everything must go, and in place of all these holidays we'll celebrate Great Historical Figures Day, the one day where you honor whichever historical person you choose. Prefer Booker T. Washington over Martin Luther King?

Honor Booker. Think Washington and Lincoln were overrated and America's greatest President was Ronald Reagan? Honor the Gipper and his trickle-down theory. Believe our leaders are all just feeble puppets of an all-powerful New World Order? Honor the Illuminati and their death-like grip on our country's banking system. Or honor them all. It doesn't matter. Just think about history and don't go to work.

February – Monday after the Super Bowl – Lennon's Day

Valentine's Day, you're out. I'm fine with turning a sacred idea like love into a consumerist Hallmark holiday, but I can't support a day where the goal is to drive all single girls to suicide. Imagine if you made a holiday where all races got to celebrate, except Native Americans had to sit in the dark and cry. That's basically what Valentine's Day is, but in this case Native Americans are 24-year-old brunettes in sweatpants with ice cream all over their face. I care too much about single girls to condone that sort of thing. So instead, we replace it with Lennon's Day, a day where we celebrate love in all its forms, be it a relationship with a spouse or the love you share with your best friend. Of course we'll name this day after John Lennon, the number one all-time advocate of love. I toyed with the idea of making the daytime part of this holiday called Lennon's Day and the nighttime part called Paris Hilton Night, because we all know where love leads to, but I think we'll just stick with Lennon's Day. And it will occur the day after the Super Bowl, because let's be honest, no one is productive on that day anyway.

March – Date TBD – St. Patrick's Day

Why is the date TBD, you ask? St. Patrick's Day is a day of debauchery, filled with lots of young people drinking heavily and screaming loudly. That's why we need to line it up with the beginning of the NCAA Tournament. Each March, the first Thursday and Friday of the Tourney will also double as St. Patrick's Day(s). That way everyone can stay home, watch the games, and get absolutely plastered for 4 days in a row. You're not an alcoholic, you're just celebrating culture!

April – First Friday – Good Easter Friday

I don't understand why Easter switches dates every year. Did Jesus die on a bunch of different days? I shouldn't have to get out a computer or a calculator to figure out when Easter is going to occur. Let's pick one weekend and be done with it. Oh, and is Good Friday a holiday or not? Apparently it was good enough for our Lord and Savior to die and begin the process of a resurrection into everlasting life, but it's not good enough for me to get off work. So either America hates Jesus or we're not marketing this day the way we should. Listen, Jesus knew what he was doing. He could've had that Last Supper any time, but he chose to have it on Thursday night because he wanted to have Friday free for other things. That's why we must give everyone the first Friday of April off, and honor Easter for three days straight, the way Jesus intended. When you drink yourself into oblivion on the new Good Easter Friday, you'll have plenty of time to chug Gatorade and rise from the dead.

May – Last Monday – Soldiers' Day

I hope this doesn't seem like an insult to our troops, but I don't see the need for Memorial Day AND Veterans' Day. They can be combined. Remember, the more holidays you have, the less each one means. Do you want America to give you two hand jobs, or would you rather she fucked your brains out once? Alright then. Memorial Day is the start to summer, and Veteran's Day is in cold November, so let's honor our soldiers on the day when all Americans are happy and warm. With that summertime association we'll never forget how our troops keep the sun shining on America's freedom, or how hot a man in uniform can be. So let's get pumped for our soldiers — and kick off summer right — once a year at the end of May.

June – Third Friday – Families Day

Mother's Day. Father's Day. That's two trips to the Hallmark store in less than a month, and if you're like me, not a single feeling of warmth or compassion toward a loved one. "I have to go to the store and buy ANOTHER card? Stupid parents!" Also, recent trends suggest that by the year 2036 no one will actually have a mother AND a father. Once again, let's combine holidays and have a day where we celebrate our entire family, and oh yeah, one that doesn't fall on a day we already have off from work.

July 4th – Independence Day

There's no need to fuck with Fourth of July. Hot dogs, burgers, fireworks, and beer? It's like God himself invented this holiday. Then He must have shot himself in the head with a bottle rocket, because I don't know what He was thinking when He came up with Flag Day. What a crock of shit that "holiday" is. Oh, let's honor a piece of cloth. Awesome. Betsy Ross, suck my balls. Fourth of July honors America 1000x times better than Flag Day ever could, by celebrating all the things that make America great: Good times with family and friends, honor and patriotism, and mass consumption of potato salad and Bud Light. America, bitches!

August – Third Friday – Brock Stele Day

One summer when I was on break from college, I coached my little brother's softball team. I didn't want to be the only person over 18, so I convinced my friend Jeremy to play on the team under the pseudonym "Brock Stele." (It was an 18-and-under league and Jeremy was 20, hence the fake persona.) Since no one knew Brock Stele, we were able to make up ridiculous lies about his back story. We told our teammates that Brock was studying to become a nuclear physicist by day, while training for the Olympic curling team at night. We said that he moved here from Saskatchewan and planned on joining the Peace Corps and heading to Africa upon graduation. After the season ended, I ran into a couple girls from the team, and when they asked what Brock was up to, I told them he had died in a spelunking accident in the mountains of South America.

Anyway, the point is, we need a holiday in August. There's nothing the entire month and it sucks. C'mon man, we're in the middle of summer and we can't get a government-mandated day off? It's bullshit. That's why, under my calendar, we would take a day each August to celebrate Brock Stele Day, a holiday dedicated to dreamers and risk-takers. America was founded by courageous men who took extraordinary action, and there should be a holiday celebrating the citizens of this great nation who stray from the flock and overcome great odds to improve their lives and make this country a better place. So enjoy Brock Stele Day, and please, celebrate responsibly.

September 11th – America Day

9/11 is the most appalling thing to happen in this country, but the second most appalling thing is that we haven't yet made it an official holiday. Congress created the label "Patriot Day" back in 2001, but that moniker is far too divisive, given the Patriot Act and the newfound political undertones of the word "patriot." Instead, we should create a new holiday, "America Day." This would be a chance to both honor victims of the tragedy, and to remind our enemies that we aren't fucking around and that all who attack the United States will eventually be captured and prison-raped by the most awesome county in the history of mankind.

September – Last Monday – Working Class Heroes Day

You might be wondering, "What happened to Labor Day?" Well, it's been pushed back. We all know Labor Day serves as the unofficial end to summer. The first weekend of September is already too early to end summer, and if this global warming thing is for real, then we're going to want to think about extending Labor Day until late September at least. Also, let me explain the name change. Labor Day should be a celebration of all working class people, but these days the term "labor" only brings to mind unions and pregnant chicks. Labor Day should celebrate everyone! Actually, it should celebrate everyone EXCEPT pregnant chicks. Get back to work, you lazy fatasses! Anyway, Working Class Heroes Day sounds cooler, and it would be a day to celebrate all the great hardworking men and women in this country. If you put in extra hours every week... if you don't have a trust fund... if you are stuck in a cubicle right now... if you own no more than two suits and you got them from Men's Wearhouse... you are a Working Class Hero! Now enjoy your day off work.

October – Third Monday – Ethnicity Day

I have nothing against Columbus Day. I also have nothing for Columbus Day. I don't think I've ever gotten it off, or gone to a Columbus Day party, or made out with a drunk girl on Columbus Day. You know what that means. Sorry Chris Columbus, but you're cut. Instead, we replace this day with Ethnicity Day, a day when we can take all of those annoying ethnic-based parades that happen throughout the year and get them all out of the way on one action-packed afternoon. Puerto Ricans, Jamaicans, Argentineans, Chinese, and Canadians... everyone gets a parade! Italians can continue with their Columbus celebration too. Even the gays can get in on this. Have a parade, show your pride, yell out anti-homophobic chants, go nuts! Ethnicity Day is a chance for everyone to get together with their people and celebrate diversity, specifically why your diversity is better than everyone else's diversity. And the best part is, everyone gets the day off work. Except police. We'll need them for the Puerto Rican parade.

November – Last Thursday – Thanksgiving

There's no need to change Thanksgiving, but I would like to add a federal mandate regarding the Wednesday before Thanksgiving. For anyone between the ages of 18 and 30, this is its own holiday. So when my plan goes into effect, all business must shut down at 3pm on the day before Thanksgiving, and may not reopen until Friday morning. That way, young adults will have a chance to rest up before they go out, get drunk, and hit on some girl from high school that they haven't seen in 6 years but got pretty cute while she was away at college.

December 25th – Christmas

Again, not a lot of reason to mess around with Christmas. I do hate when Christmas falls on a weekend, but I guess you can't change the date, seeing as how it's Santa's birthday and all. So enjoy the final holiday of the year, and remember, 'tis better to get wasted than to receive!

20
8 Reasons I Love McDonald's

McDonald's is a landmark of this great nation of ours, but it seems like recently, the tide has been turning against the fast food giant. America is emerged in a health craze, and Micky D's has become public enemy #1.

It doesn't help that, just a few years back, the movie *Super Size Me* gave an extremely unflattering look at the company and the ramifications that come with eating too much of its food.

I think it's time to take a stand against this negativity. I love McDonald's. It's quick, it's cheap, and it's delicious. However, it seems like every time I sit down to eat a feast from the Golden Arches, someone tries to deter me from enjoying my meal. They all say the same thing:

"How can you eat that stuff? You need to watch that movie *Super Size Me*. You'll never want to touch McDonald's again!"

My response is always the same:

"I'll eat McDonald's *while* I watch that movie. Then when it's over, I'll eat more. Now get out of here."

I'm not going to stand around while some "documentary" filmmaker and a bunch of health nuts tarnish an

American tradition. Here are 8 reasons why I love McDonald's...

1) The Dollar Menu

The Dollar Menu isn't only the cheapest food at McDonald's. It's also the best. The McChicken sandwich is amazing. The cheeseburgers are great. The mozzarella sticks are sublime. Even that thing that looks like a little gyro is solid (I don't know what it is and I don't care). You can get a full meal for 3 bucks. At some places you can't even get a bottled water for that much.

2) McFlurry's

McFlurry's are delicious. Oreo McFlurry's are the best, but M&M McFlurry's are no slouch either. Eating a McFlurry is like being in a fairytale where you're sitting on a unicorn next to a naked supermodel. Except better, because everyone knows that people in fairytales never get to fuck. In conclusion, they should have never gotten rid of the Reese's Pieces McFlurry.

3) The Employees

Laugh if you want, but McDonald's employees are light years beyond the employees at other fast food restaurants. You go to Taco Bell or KFC and it's 50/50 the person even understood your order. You said you wanted "2 chalupa's and one soft taco," and all they heard was "get me a Pepsi with some urine please." Not cause they're the type of rude employees that would urinate in a soda, but because their English is honestly that bad. McDonald's employees, on the other hand, are like machines. I don't know what the training regimen at Mickey D's entails, but when compared to the legions of other fast food chains, those guys have their shit together. McDonald's employees work as a perfect assembly line, quickly churning out burgers and obeying the orders of their amazing master, you, the customer. McDonald's employees are what the Nazis would have been like if they were using their powers toward deliciousness instead of evil.

4) Double Cheeseburgers

Eating one is good. Eating two is incredible. Eating three will literally kill you. I always eat two. Except that one time, when I ate three and went into a coma for 20 minutes. Luckily I had ordered *four*, and I gave the last one to God in exchange for a second chance at life. God was all like, "what, no fries?," but I said, "hey man, I only had four bucks!" I totally had more though. Whatever, screw that guy.

5) The Game Room

Sure, you're probably too old now, but remember how much fun McDonald's was as a kid? You don't get to go down a slide into a pile of plastic balls at Applebee's, I'll tell you that much. Some McDonald's franchises even have video games now. You go for lunch, you get to play Xbox. Amazing, right? As a kid, you can't pass up that kind of opportunity. And it's genius on the part of McDonald's, because that's how they hook so many kids on the food for life. I actually tried a similar business plan when I put a Nintendo Wii on top of a cigarette dispenser. It was working pretty well until these two guys from the government showed up and took all the cigarettes away. Our government doesn't support small businesses, man.

6) They're everywhere

If I have to drive 2 miles to find a McDonald's, that probably means I'm at the North Pole. Anywhere else, you can throw a football and hit one — if not two — McDonald's franchises. That means Mickey D's is always an option. I could be starving in a strange town in Nova Scotia, but it doesn't matter, because I know there's at least one familiar option in town. "Hmm, what should I have tonight... how about McDonald's?" Those words have been uttered many times by many wise men. Confucius had his journey of 1,000 miles. Moses had his trip through the desert. Neither of them died of starvation, did they? Why do think that is? Cause there are McDonald's fucking everywhere. And it's all the same. The chicken nuggets meal in Hollywood is the same as the chicken nuggets meal in New York. McDonald's is like a nice warm fireplace, making you feel right at home, even if you're lost in some shithole in the Dakotas.

7) The food is terrible for you

Here's why I hate that *Super Size Me* movie. First off, the guy only got one shot at making the film. A movie where he turned out fine would have been boring, so you know he's hamming it up the whole time. More importantly, he eats McDonald's every meal for a month. Well of course you're going to nearly die. McDonald's is a treat, meant to be enjoyed only on occasion. It's supposed to be bad. That's the point. You get it when you're in a rush, or are traveling, or just don't feel like cooking. But not every day. I mean, if you went around having unprotected sex every day, you wouldn't complain when you caught the clap, would you? Of course not, you'd realize you're an idiot and stop it. All intelligent people know that it's best to have McDonald's and unprotected sex once or twice a week, max.

8) It makes stupid people fat

This ties into the point above. Some people are too dumb to realize that McDonald's should be enjoyed in moderation. And you know what happens to those people? You guessed it. They get fat. There's no need for anyone to complain about McDonald's, because it already has its own built-in punishment. You eat too much, you get fat. You eat even more, you have a heart attack and die. It's natural selection at its finest.

And that's why I love McDonald's. Because McFlurry's taste good and it kills fat people. The end.

21
My Plan to Dominate the Music Industry

Becoming an international music sensation is tough. Few acts can achieve that level of success based on talent alone. That's why you see things like Katy Perry flashing her breasts, or Lady Gaga dressing like a crazy person, or tons of young musicians trying to be the next Free Credit Report spokesband. They know that they need to do something beyond just playing songs in order to be noticed. Oh sure, you can break through based solely on talent, but that's extremely rare. For every Radiohead, there are 80,000 Jonas Brothers; for every Notorious B.I.G., a million Soulja Boys.

However, there is one way to greatly increase your chances of success, and it's something that few of the posturing young wanna-be's in the music industry have picked up on.

The secret is to sing about a specific place. Whether it's Tupac's "California Love," Jay-Z's "Empire State of Mind," or even Katy Perry's "Waking Up in Vegas," songs about locations have been monstrously successfully throughout the ages. People have a certain pride not only about their hometown, but about places that are near and dear to their heart. You may live in Norwalk, Connecticut, but that doesn't mean you can't feel a sense of hometown pride when Jay-Z raps about the New York Yankees. Hell, you could be in Iowa, but when Weezer sings about living the high life in Beverly Hills, your inner movie star is awakened and you feel like the song is speaking to you personally. We don't even need to get into country songs. Based on country songs, you'd think Nashville was Mecca, not just some place where rednecks drink PBR and do choreographed dances while wearing rattlesnake ties.

Sadly, most songs written about cities are written about MAJOR cities. That's where I come in. My plan is to record a bunch of songs about America's mediocre-to-crappy locations, and then make a killing by selling those songs to the residents of whatever city the song happens to be about.

Take a look at how many songs have been written about New York City. Or check out the myriad songs written about Los Angeles or Las Vegas. Miami has been the subject of a plethora of hits. All of America's major cities have had a ballad or two written in their honor. But what about this nation's lesser cities? Nobody's writing songs about Lincoln, Nebraska. No artists care enough to dedicate a rock anthem to Tuscaloosa, Alabama. Who will write a song for Binghamton, New York?

I will.

By writing a ton of generic songs about Butte, Montana or Tempe, Arizona, I will capitalize off of people's local pride and everyone's desire to be mentioned in lyrical form. I'll rise to the top of the music industry by championing Pierre, North Dakota and Sheboygan, Wisconsin.

I know what you're thinking: Nobody gives a fuck about Wisconsin. While you are correct in the macro sense, you're also totally wrong in the micro sense. If there was a song called "Sheboygan is the Best Place Ever," everybody in Sheboygan, Wisconsin would download that fucking song. I'm assuming people in Wisconsin have learned how to download music. It's 2011. They must know how to download music, right? Yeah, anyway, this is going to make me rich.

Everything has become splintered since the rise of the Internet. Whether it's TV, music, or movies, there are fewer smash hits and more and more cult favorites. You take away Barack Obama, Lady Gaga, and xenophobia, and it's hard to find anything that all Americans collectively share. These days it's much better to have a small legion of devoted followers than a semi-large audience of indifferent kids with ADHD. That's why my plan is genius. I'll simultaneously create thousands of small cult followings for my songs about crappy... I mean, underappreciated cities. By pandering to the unwashed masses one town at a time, I'll make a name for myself and gain unfathomable riches. People in Albuquerque, New Mexico will rock out to my power ballad "I Can't Spell Albuquerque (But That Don't Mean I Don't Love It)" while folks in Baton Rouge, Louisiana sway along with my acoustic jam "Hey Baton Rouge, I'm Sure You're Cool But I Honestly Don't Know A Single Thing About Your City So I'm Just Going To Say 'Baton Rouge' and 'Yeah' A Lot." I mean, if Beyonce can sing about her "single ladies" when she's been married for years, then why can't I sing about the grandiose beauty of a bunch of shitty towns I would never visit?

You loved it when Big and Rich were coming to your city. Well I'm coming to your city, playing a crappy power ballad about your city, taking a bunch of money from your city, and then leaving your city for someplace cooler. What's not to love? You get to feel good about yourself, I get to become rich and famous, and... well... I guess that's it. So give me your money, small-town assholes, and I'll see you in hell. By which I mean your city, on my world tour.

22
The Meaning of Life, Part III

I love answering deep hypothetical questions with overly-obvious, literal responses.

Say someone asks me the meaning of life. I would look them right in the eye and say, "It's finding love. Everyone knows that."

Or, to give you a real-life example, a few years ago I was in Washington D.C. and a bartender wanted to know if I believed a man should be exempt from state and federal laws while completely within his own property. In other words, he asked me, "If I were inside a room, on my own property, with no doors and no windows, unseen by the outside world, with my actions not affecting anyone except myself, should I still be considered a citizen subject to the arbitrary and inherently unfair rules of a country, or rather an individual subject only to my own beliefs and values?"

Without hesitation and as seriously as possible, I responded:

"I believe you should shut up and get me another Bud Light."

You could say I'm not giving the right answers, but really, people just aren't asking the right questions.

23
Tom Z For President

My fellow Americans,

I, Tom Z, am writing to announce my candidacy for the Presidency in the year 2016. I feel it is my civic duty to run for President, and I am honored to have the opportunity to win your vote.

In these times of economic and social crisis, it is imperative that we elect a leader that represents the best interests of you, the American public. That is why I'm running for President. Like you, I am disgusted by these Washington insiders who work solely for the special interest groups. Our country needs massive change, a change that can only come from the outside. The "old boys club" on Capitol Hill needs to be eliminated, and we need a President who represents the views of the common man.

I am that candidate.

Like you, I understand the pressures of a failing economy and the toll that war has taken on our great country. Like you, I care more about being able to pay for groceries than being able to pay the big oil companies. Like you, I'm annoyed by the greed on Wall Street which affects all of us on Main Street. Like you, I can't stand to witness the same old party politics while so many people struggle to pay their mortgages. Like you, I despise our shallow values and celebrity-driven culture, and like you, I believe that Lindsay Lohan's comeback totally isn't going to happen cause she's, like, still all crazy and obsessed with her ex-boyfriend. Like you, I struggle with contractions and don't understand the difference between "your" and "you're." And just like you, I care deeply about our country and you're children's future.

You see, I'm just like you. I'm a man of the people. I'm not some Washington D.C. fat cat who has been entrenched on Capitol Hill for years and is out of touch with the rest of the country. I'm no Washington insider. In fact I've only been to Washington once in my life, and that was when I was 13 years old, when my mom took me to see to see the Washington Monument. And you know what? I thought it was overrated. I know it has great symbolic value, but it's just a pointy statue in the middle of some park. You can't climb up it and it doesn't even have a gift shop. What's the big deal? And don't get me started on the Lincoln Memorial. What a piece of shit.

Screw Washington D.C. and its fancy cars and shiny marble floors and phallic-shaped "monuments." I don't care about Washington. I care about you! That's why I'm running for President. We need a leader who shares the values of the average American, and who understands the struggles that we all go through on a daily basis. I am that leader. I don't go to fancy yacht parties or fact-finding missions in Darfur. I go to work every morning and bind and collate sales reports for a marketing team at a company that sells axle-rods to the riding lawnmower industry. I don't read the Wall Street Journal and trade stocks. I read *US Weekly* and trade sarcastic barbs about Kim Kardashian's vagina. Actually, I don't even know how to read. I just look at the pictures and assume the worst. I'm not some stuck up Washington elitist who believes in rainbows and butterflies and reading and economic stimulus packages!

I won't try to impress you with creative speeches or clever rhetoric. I know you're sick of all the political spin that has dominated our country for the past two decades, so I won't try to make your head hurt by saying lots of sentences with tons of big words in them. I care too much about you, the American public! Plus, I'm borderline illiterate. Some people have called me functionally retarded, but in reality my IQ is a solid 86.2, putting me right on par with the average Walmart shopper.

Did I mention I shop at Walmart? Yep, I'm just like you. Oh, those Washington D.C. fat cats have tried to take me to fancy stores like Crate & Barrel or Pier 1, but I looked them right in the eyes and said to them, "What are you, a faggot?" Because that's how I feel the average American would've handled the situation, and I'll be damned if I let these party politics affect me from doing my job of serving the American people! This has earned me quite the reputation around Washington as a "renegade." Just as Rage Against the Machine were renegades of funk, I'm the renegade of Washington. But that's OK, because I know that I don't work for other politicians or Rage Against the Machine. I work for you! I shop at Walmart and I buy my pretzels in 20-gallon jars because we are in a recession!

I may be running for President, but I take offense to the word politician. I'm no politician. I'm just an ordinary guy. I didn't go to politician school or pass some magical politician test. I can't even spell the word politician without help from my computer's spellcheck function. I dropped out of school in eighth grade to work in my family's shipping and packaging business, bubble-wrapping dinette sets for average Americans just like you. As President, I promise to bubble-wrap our country and protect you from the ill effects of an economy that has been kicked around in the back of a UPS truck. I promise to submerge terrorists into a refrigerator box filled with Styrofoam peanuts, until they have inhaled massive amounts of asbestos and are no longer able to plot attacks against America. I promise to hand-deliver a better America by 8AM on a Saturday morning without requesting a signature, while speaking in vague metaphors that don't really make sense but can be interpreted however you, the American people, choose!

By electing me President, you'll be scoring a touchdown for progress! Because like you, I'm a huge sports fan, and believe that athletes deserve the type of admiration and respect that hypothetically should be reserved for teachers and law enforcement. I'm not some Washington elitist who thinks that all laws need to be upheld! I occasionally jaywalk, just like you! Sometimes I fall behind on my credit card bills and write them angry letters saying I never got my statement that month, even though I did get it and just couldn't afford to pay. One time I got hammered and drove home from the bar and struck a small child with my SUV. I didn't stop to see what happened, but I found out the next day that the kid had died. Mothers Against Drunk Driving went on the local news and demanded that the perpetrator turn himself in, but I never told anyone what I did. Why? Because I don't cater to the special interest groups!

The old boys club in Washington goes out to $1,000

dinners to discuss politics as usual. I, on the other hand, don't play that game. I usually eat cut up hot dogs that I dump into a bowl of mac and cheese. Once in awhile I treat myself to Arby's. I occasionally steal the sports section of my neighbor's newspaper, and when he asks about it, I play dumb, like, "I don't know what you're talking about, Jim." I don't shower on Sundays and just hose myself down with Axe Body Spray. I often pick my nose in public and I've been known to cut in front of old ladies in the supermarket check-out line. It's 3PM, I just woke up, and in a few more hours I'll be blackout drunk on low-grade grain alcohol. I go to bars and hit on woman and it's really creepy. I don't pay my taxes and I haven't given my ex-wife her court-ordered alimony in 6 months. I refuse to participate in such fiscal irresponsibility, and as President, I would lower everyone's taxes by 50% while simultaneously investing billions of dollars into infrastructure and sunshine. Of course, I'll need a calculator to figure out all this economic stuff, because like you, I fuckin' hate math! It's boring and I never really got it. I'm not huge on science or history, either! This isn't high school, it's the school of America!

The other day I met a group of young parents at a diner. I told them I was running for President, and one of the young mothers asked me, "Are you high? Leave me alone!" It's sad that we live in a country where drug use is so prevalent that this mother would just assume I was high. I can't stand the fact that we've become so divided by party politics that this woman would sooner ask me to leave her alone than discuss the real issues facing America.

I'm running for President in order to make a change. As

President, I'll take the lead from the American public and stop succumbing to pressure from the big drug companies. In fact, I'll take all medicine out of stores and lock all doctors into concentration camps. We don't need those fat cats charging us $75 then telling us to just rest up and take some Advil. Not in this economy!

You might be asking, "Tom, why are you announcing your candidacy for President five years before the 2016 election, especially when there's another election coming up in 2012?" The answer is simple. I don't know anything about politics. I don't understand the political process or how to campaign or even how to fill out the necessary paperwork in order to officially enter the Presidential race. That's because I'm not some elitist Washington insider who participates in party politics or knows his own social security number.

I'm just an ordinary guy, like you. That's right, I'm a goddamn idiot. And together, we can turn this country into the America we all want. An America where the economy is stable, an America where everyone can afford gasoline and adequate healthcare, an America where we're not engaged in a never-ending war, an America where pints are a dollar and everybody gets laid!

Vote Tom Z in 2016! Together, we can make good things happen! For me! And then maybe for you! If there's time! Yeah! Vote for me or Mexicans will eat your children! God Bless America!!!

24
Black People Are the New White People

The most important figure in the history of civil rights is Martin Luther King, Jr.

The second most important figure?

Kanye West.

Oh sure, others have a strong case. Lincoln freed the slaves, but someone was bound to free them eventually. Rosa Parks' refusal to move to the back of the bus was symbolic of the entire civil rights movement, but she wasn't the only one to take a stand against segregation practices. She simply received the most attention. Plus, how do we know she wasn't just lazy? Malcolm X was a proud black leader, but let's be honest, no one under 35 can name one thing he ever did. He's only famous because he has a cool name. Harriett Tubman did a great job leading the Underground Railroad, but she lacked the sex appeal to sway the media and get shit done on a national level. Seriously Tubman, would it kill you to put on a little foundation?

And that leaves us with Kanye.

On a serious note, I truly believe that Kanye West has done more for civil rights over the past decade than anyone.

From the late 1980s until the early 2000s, rap music

focused on the gangster lifestyle. Never has there been a more aptly-name genre of music than "Gangsta Rap." Rappers like N.W.A., Tupac, Notorious B.I.G., Dr. Dre, and 50 Cent spearheaded the gangsta movement, and thousands of lesser known rappers helped perpetuate the image of guns, drugs, and bitches. The genre focused on themes like hustling, dealing drugs, shooting your enemies, and refusing to obey authorities. Hardcore rap fans were told to "stop snitchin'." They learned to say "fuck tha police." They were informed that "bitches ain't shit but hoes and tricks." And everybody knew that "you don't want to fuck with Shady, cause Shady will fucking kill you."

Say what you will about art imitating life, but it's hard to argue that certain people aren't drawn to certain music. How many fans of the Cure do you see whistling and skipping down the street? Do you notice a lot of Slipknot fans at the yoga studio? How many Rhodes Scholars own a Soulja Boy album? You think many Coldplay fans beat their wives?

I'm joking around of course. Nobody likes Coldplay. The point is, many of the people listening to gangsta rap were envious of the gangsta lifestyle. I know, I know, 70% of the people buying rap albums are rich white kids from the suburbs. But that still leaves another 30% that consists mostly of impressionable, impoverished young minorities. We're talking about millions of black and Hispanic teenagers who, from the early '90s until the early '00s, looked up to role models such as Tupac, Biggie, and 50 Cent. These rappers spoke frequently about violence and drugs. While I can't argue with Fiddy's beats, Biggie's flow, or Tupac's passion, I can argue that their lyrical content was damaging to the psyche of many impressionable young black males.

Not only that, but these rappers made popular a certain style of clothing. Sweatpants, jerseys, huge jackets, oversized clothing, and Timberland boots were all in vogue for young black males. Remember FUBU jerseys? They were comically oversized jerseys that looked incredibly stupid, but they were popular thanks in no small part to the gangsta rap culture that permeated our society.

You are judged by the way you dress and act. That's a fact of life and there's no way around it. You might think that's unfair. Well too bad. That's the way it is. When young black males dressed in oversized clothing, covered themselves in tattoos, and talked about guns and drugs, they eliminated a wealth of possibilities from their future. They didn't "dress for success"; they dressed for hustlin' and hustlin' is what they got.

Bill Cosby is one of the few black role models to speak out publicly against the gangsta lifestyle. Cosby has frequently said that black people need to get an education, dress better, speak more eloquently, and stop blaming the white man for all their problems. What he's essentially saying is that they need to ditch the gangsta look and mentality. Cosby was shunned for these beliefs. When he delivered a scathing critique of young black culture in 2004, he was decried as a heretic for his views. He was a racist. He was an old man who didn't "get it." He was an Uncle Tom.

Well, Bill Cosby was right. People in America base decisions on first impressions. Most people look at someone in baggy clothes, with their pants pulled down, and immediately deem that person unprofessional and unworthy of being given any real opportunities. Are all young black people gangsta? Obviously not. But a lot of young black males were. That's not to say that type of person doesn't deserve equality or basic human rights, but you certainly won't get offered a decent job when you dress like a thug. That goes for people of every race, by the way. Bill Cosby tried to spread that message, but his voice was ignored.

Kanye wasn't, though. Instead of giving a speech about not showing your underwear, Kanye let his talent do the talking. In a time when others were rapping about doing crack and being shot, Kanye released tracks about Jesus, self-esteem, and optimism. Normally that stuff is lame, but when can put it to a beat like "Jesus Walks" then people will bump that shit in their Honda Civic and the message will eventually seep into their brains. Through his lyrics, Kanye encouraged young black people to believe in themselves, to embrace their individuality, to have faith, and to treat each other with respect. His introspective rhymes were a breath of fresh air in an era when self-promotional bragging was the norm. Granted, Kanye does his share of bragging, and he loves rapping about fucking girls, but his brags carry an "if I can do it, you can do it" sort of tone and he fucks chicks respectfully and with an aura of dignity. Kanye almost singlehandedly brought an end to the gangsta rap era, and he paved the way for a brand of thoughtful, creative rap music that is omnipresent today.

Just as important as his lyrics is the fact that, with his skyrocketing popularity, Kanye was able to change fashion. Kanye was known for bold and unique fashion choices, such as argyle sweater vests and purple tuxedos.

He wore the kind of stuff that you would see in Milan or Paris, not in the ghettos of Detroit. Yet because of his celebrity, he was able to get young black kids all over the country to ditch the FUBU jerseys and the Timbaland boots and to start dressing like fashionistas. Make no mistake about it, this gained young black males immeasurable respect, not only from their peers, but from within.

Dress in sweatpants for a week and see what happens to your self-esteem. It's hard to feel good about yourself when you're dressed like you haven't gotten out of bed. There's a reason we ask salespeople to wear suits on a sales call. It's because they'll receive a level of respect from clients that they wouldn't get if they were wearing a Charles Oakley throwback jersey. Nightclubs enforce dress codes because they believe it will help maintain a certain level of civility and class in their establishment. Unfortunately the Jersey Shore crowd is able to fuck that up, but on paper the clubs are correct. The way you present yourself will play a major factor in determining the level of success that you achieve. When you dress and act like a gangsta, you're creating a certain path for yourself. That path does not include becoming CEO of a Fortune 500 company.

In the '90s, Tupac sang that America "ain't ready to see a black President," and he was right. Although we'd come a long way since the Civil Rights movement of the 1960s, we still held many stereotypes that prevented us as a nation from electing a black man to the highest office in the land. But then Kanye came along, and now we have our country's first black President in Barack Obama. Is it a coincidence? I honestly don't think so. No one can win the Presidency without receiving a lot of votes from moderate and conservative white people. These white people were scared by gangsta rap and the youth culture associated with the genre. Then Kanye spearheaded a movement in which young black people started dressing better and acting with more self-respect. Conservative white people noticed this sea change in black youth culture and many started abandoning their prejudices. The result was an increased respect and admiration for young black people and their culture. And in this new "post-racial" atmosphere (as it's come to be called), white people were able to pull the lever for Barack Obama and make history in the unending fight for civil rights. I guess what I'm saying is, Barack Obama wouldn't be President if white people didn't love "Golddigger."

Yes, thanks in no small part to Kanye West, black people were able to overcome dangerous cultural stereotypes, improve their collective career prospects, and grasp the highest office in all the land.

It's been a great decade.

Of course, there is a Y-axis to this sociological graph:

White people.

Over the last ten years, white people have fallen to a new depth of pathetic-ness that I never dreamed possible.

First off, we wear sweatpants everywhere. I was at the mall the other day and a third of the people there were wearing sweatpants. This was on a weekday. Those of us who still have too much respect to wear sweatpants in public have done the next worst thing. We've taken all other fabrics and made them sweatpants-esque. Let's examine khakis. At some point we decided that ironing pants is too much work. So we created wrinkle-free khakis. OK. Then we decided we were spilling too many soft drinks on our pants, so we made khakis that were water repellant. Don't worry about spilling Red Bull on your crotch… it will glide right off and that 2000% of a daily sugar serving will end up on the floor. Whatever, it's the janitor's problem now! Finally we went the distance and created nylon pants that look like khakis. These are essentially the same things that NBA teams wear during pre-game warm-ups, but they're khaki colored and have a built-in crease to fool people into thinking that you're a normal human who dresses respectfully. I have a pair of nylon khakis and I used to wear them to work until one day I put them in the dryer for too long and they melted. That's a true story. I'm telling you this just so you know I'm not above the problem. My grandfather always used to tell me, "you can be a part of the problem or you can be a part of the solution." Well I took his advice and now I'm a huge part of the problem. Thanks Grandpa!

Up top for us honkies, it's all hooded sweatshirts and long-sleeved tees. There's nothing wrong with either of these items except for the fact that we wear the same ones over and over. Every white person I know owns one or two hooded sweatshirts and wears them every other day. So you end up going through like 30 wearings before washing it. And our "classy" shirts are made by Ed Hardy and have dragons and tattoos all over them. I know in the '90s people wore flannel every day, but at least a flannel shirt has buttons and a collar.

Shoes are going downhill as well. I never thought I'd see

the day when non-retarded adults were wearing Velcro shoes, but here we are in 2011 and "Velcro Nikes" returns 425,000 results in a Google search. Like any Google search 20% of those results are weird Velcro-related porn sites, but that's still a lot of lazy sneaker wearers. I love sneakers but I've never thought, "These stringy things are too difficult to tie together." Slippers have become a huge commodity, and for those who think slippers are too classy, there are hundreds of different variations of Crocs you can buy for all your white-trash needs. The most popular brand of boot is Uggs, which are basically a raccoon pelt that's been turned inside-out. White people also replaced their loafers with slip-on dress shoes. These may look the same as our old dress shoes, but by eliminating the laces we've eliminated our need to ever think or do anything.

Do I need to bring up Snuggies? Pajama Jeans? Trucker hats? Jeggings? The Jimmy Fallon haircut? The point is that us white people have gotten remarkably lazy when it comes to presenting ourselves. It's not a few isolated incidents or a small white-trash segment of the population. It's all of us. We just don't care anymore. We'll take any piece of clothing and try to secretly convert it into pajamas. We use terms like "water-resistant" and "athletic" to make it seem like we're taking a step forward, but in reality we're just justifying our desire to wear pajamas at all times. It's only a matter of time before we're seeing nylon business suits and sweat-tuxedos. That's when we'll know we've hit rock-bottom. Fortunately rock bottom will be made out of leopard-print fleece so it will be a nice soft landing.

It's sad. As black people are ascending toward the top of Dr. King's mountain in their Prada hiking boots, white people are base jumping off the cliff in Crocs and a pre-ripped Abercrombie parachute. I always knew black people could reach such heights. I just assumed white people would still be there to hang out with them when they did. Experts predict that over the next 20 years we'll see a massive shift in the cultural makeup of America, and that white people will become the new minority. I say we're already there.

25
Smart People Are the New Idiots

There was a time when it was easy to tell smart people and dumb people apart. Smart people got good grades, aced the SATs, went off to Ivy League colleges, and became the most successful lawyers and doctors of their generation. They cured disease, developed mathematical formulas, and worked to change the laws of our nation. Dumb people, meanwhile, skipped class and usually ended up barely graduating from high school. They went on to work low-paying and unglamorous jobs, building the foundation of your house, fixing your toilet, and pumping your gas.

Back then, intelligence and stupidity had narrowly defined roles.

But alas, a new day has dawned.

And for that, you can thank technology.

For starters, there's no reason to ever learn anything these days. With the click of a mouse, you can Google the answer to any question. Remember fifteen years ago when someone would ask, "Who was that guy…" and your friends would spend the next twenty minutes trying to recall the old singer who campaigned for freedom of speech in rap music? (John Denver.) Back then, there was an incentive to learn things, because you could answer peoples' questions and appear to be intelligent. Now that conversation would never occur, because within ten seconds someone would have looked it up on their smartphone. Today the way to impress people is by Googling something faster than the guy next to you.

Intelligent people think that their vast knowledge of the web and technology makes them smarter, but that's not necessarily true. If you spend all day on science websites reading about DNA reconstruction, you will probably end up more intelligent. Of course, we're not doing that. We're on Facebook and Twitter, messaging our friends. We're on Amazon.com searching for discounts on shoes that we probably won't buy. We're on IMDB.com, trying to find out the name of that guy who's in every movie. (James Rebhorn.) We're absorbing more information, but that information isn't useful in any way beyond the present moment.

And that's how smart people have become the new idiots. We do more than ever, yet we don't accomplish nearly as much as we used to.

When the Internet started becoming mainstream, news organizations made a critical choice. They decided that delivering information quickly and producing a higher quantity of news was more important than producing quality content and useful information. I don't know why the whole world decided to go along with this, but we did. We now have news sources battling for page views, and striving to put out as many stories as they can as quickly as possible. The decline in quality news and the financial problems caused by this strategy have been covered ad nauseum. But we rarely discuss what has happened to us as consumers of the Internet. Smart people, instead of diving into issues and absorbing information, now battle to learn superficial details about as many useless topics as possible.

I don't believe that we are simply "distracted" as some people like to say. I think that we've experienced a cultural sea change in which there's now greater value placed on how many facts we can learn than on what we do with that knowledge. Think back to high school. There were the very smart kids, and then there were the kids who were good at memorizing. Every school had a few of the latter. These kids would cram the night before an exam, memorizing the answers to any questions that could possibly appear on the test. They would get an A+, and then immediately forget everything they had learned. If you asked them about the exam a week later, they couldn't tell you anything. These kids were A-students, but we all knew they weren't that smart. Thanks to technology, the world is quickly becoming a nation of memorizers. This week, we'll give you 100 facts about Charlie Sheen, and next week we'll be experts on Japanese plate tectonics, but none of that information will ever translate into anything tangible and we'll forget it just as quickly as we learned it.

Unfortunately, it's not only information itself, but also the process of acquiring knowledge that makes a person smart. Anyone can memorize data, but truly intelligent people accumulate knowledge and then use it as tool to achieve their goals. We've all heard the proverb, "Give a man a fish and you feed him for a day, but teach a man to fish and you feed him for a lifetime." Well, give a man an iPhone and he'll no longer have time to fish, because he's too busy looking up Division 3 lacrosse scores on the ESPN ScoreCenter app. In the Internet age, we've tricked ourselves into believing that being busy correlates with accomplishment, but that's not usually the case.

I'm not trying to float the age-old "things used to be better…" argument. For starters, I hate old people, so I would never give praise to past generations. The only things I give previous generations credit for are the invention of the wheel and the British Invasion. Even the wheel I'm not totally sold on. Secondly, I love websites like Facebook and Twitter, and I think they serve a valuable purpose in modern-day society. I just think that we need to place a higher value on the way people use technology, instead of celebrating the fact that they are simply using it. We're getting more and more knowledgeable, but we've stopped creating things. We've replaced imagination and creativity with consumption. If you think we're currently using technology to the fullest, you're sadly mistaken. For every Twitter, there are 1,000 cat blogs. For every Steve Jobs, there are a million people who spend all day jacking off and watching videos of people falling off treadmills. Computers are doing our old jobs, and we're not using them to create enough new jobs.

Fortunately, the world still has idiots. I never thought I'd be appreciative or envious of dumb people, but over the past decade I've slowly come to admire them.

To clarify, I believe the stereotype of an "idiot" goes like this: It's someone who barely graduated high school. They couldn't get into any decent college, so they learned a trade and got a mediocre-paying, blue collar job; something that involved manual labor, like a plumber or a mechanic. Society would look at that person as someone who underachieved in life. We might not call them idiots per se, but we wouldn't consider them smart.

I think it's time to reconsider.

As technology improves and employees become more easily replaceable, the people with the strongest job security will be those who possess a tangible skill. The "idiots" who ended up as plumbers, construction workers, landscapers, and auto mechanics are going to rule the world soon. While book-smart white-collar employees spend their time surfing the web, these blue-collar workers are out in the field, completing important jobs that keep our society running. They may not have grown up desiring these manual labor jobs. As children, none of them thought, "When I grow up, I want to remodel kitchen cabinetry!" But as luck would have it, their lack of traditional "success" may very well turn out to be a blessing in disguise. Corporate jobs can be outsourced, but it'll be a long time before you see a computer laying the foundation for a house.

You see, unlike many corporate employees, these blue-collar employees actually achieve something. I had a 97 average in high school. Since college I've had four different corporate jobs. In two of those jobs, I never produced a single tangible result. Not one. Most of my time was spent pushing paper or dealing with pointless bureaucracy. The two jobs I've enjoyed most in my life were as an online music writer and a landscaper. The former was a brief career, the latter a summer job during college. Neither of these jobs paid well and neither was considered very prestigious. But in each job I was able to create something that I could later look back on with pride, be it an article about Pearl Jam or a well-groomed lawn. I've made more money in a corporate setting, but I never considered myself as successful in those types of jobs because I didn't get the same sense of accomplishment that I got from producing something tangible. Most blue collar jobs come with that sense of accomplishment. Every carpenter has built something. Every plumber has fixed something. Every trucker has finished a long haul across the country and delivered necessary goods to a supplier.

In addition to this intrinsic job satisfaction, there's the issue of necessity. The key to success in the near future is going to be providing value. The recent recession has been a wake-up call to all white collar middle managers who command a high salary while doing very little. Technology supplies all the information we could ever ask for, and soon employees will no longer be able to get along on intelligence and knowledge alone. They'll have to produce something. Regardless of where they work, everyone will have to provide a good or service of value, or they'll quickly be replaced by a machine. Blue collar workers needn't worry about providing value, because they already do that every day. Paper-pushing white collar workers, on the other hand, should be very concerned. White collar employees can talk about "search marketing" and "branding strategies" as if they are experts, but if they aren't able to achieve results, they'll soon be out the door.

If that's not enough, the monetary tables are slowly starting to turn in favor of the blue-collar worker. Since there's now a business for everything, most middle-class people can no longer complete even the simplest of tasks. This goes back to the aforementioned learning problem of the technology age. A lot of people used to change their car's oil, but now everyone goes to Valvoline. People used to mow their own lawns, but now more and more middle-class folks are hiring landscapers. Rich people are even worse. They can't wipe their own ass without help from an assistant. We need blue-collar workers to take care of more and more tasks. Thanks to the law of supply and demand, I believe we're about to see the cost for blue collar work skyrocket in the coming years. The kids who nearly failed out of high school are about to become an irreplaceable and invaluable commodity. Meanwhile, those of us who studied our asses off will have to take lower and lower wages as we fight for the handful of computer jobs that haven't been sent over to China.

So who are the idiots now?

I guess my advice to everyone is, if you have a young child, make them put down the books and go play hours of video games instead. Every time they study, they're just helping to destroy their own future.

26
Fuckin' Squirrels

I'm a lover of animals.

Let me rephrase that.

I'm a lover of most animals.

Dogs are great. Cats are OK. Birds are interesting to watch as long as they're not shitting on your head. Cows and fish are delicious. I think dolphins are overrated but I do like them in music videos. Other animals are cool too.

But not squirrels. Squirrels are by far the worst animals. I hate them. All they're good at is chewing things and running into oncoming traffic. They fucking love running into traffic. You'd think after 87 billion squirrels were hit by cars, the squirrel race would wise up and start using crosswalks. But no. Thousands of squirrels are hit by cars every day. If squirrels were schoolchildren, 95% of them would be diagnosed as mentally challenged. They'd actually have to flip-flop the short bus with the regular bus because there would be too many special needs squirrels. It'd be like, "Hey Jimmy, I heard you have to ride the long bus to school, hahahaha, loser!" Imagine Rain Man without the good looks or the card-counting skills, and with rabies instead. That's every squirrel. How are squirrels not extinct? We should change the phrase "fucking like rabbits" to "fucking like squirrels" because clearly they must reproduce at an incredible rate to offset all their brethren who are crushed by Goodyear tires every day. What kind of stupid fucking creature does the same thing over and over despite horrific consequences? Why would any phylum of the animal kingdom continue to abuse itself day after day when there are infinite ways to avoid tragedy?

Oh well, who knows what those idiots are thinking. Stupid fuckin' squirrels. Now if you'll excuse me, I have to go to my job. I've worked there for 12 years now. It sucks and I hate my boss, but hey, it's a paycheck.

27
I am 110 Years Ahead of My Time

Back in the 1970s, Jimmy Page and Led Zeppelin had mass commercial appeal, but were constantly bashed by rock critics. Page brushed off these criticisms by declaring that the band was a year ahead of its time, and that people would eventually catch up.

In the late '90s, Billy Corgan and the Smashing Pumpkins released an album called *Adore*. The album represented the band's transition away from rock and into electronic music. It was a commercial and critical disaster. Corgan brushed off criticism by declaring that *Adore* was ten years ahead of its time, and that people wouldn't truly understand its greatness without the passage of a decade.

In the 2000s, ex-Blink182 singer Tom DeLonge started releasing music with a new band called Angels & Airwaves. The project was a vast departure from Blink, and fans and critics didn't immediately warm up to it. DeLonge brushed off criticism by declaring that Angels & Airwaves was partaking in a 30-year plan to change lives, and that the full effect of the band's music wouldn't be seen until three decades from its release.

As technology evolves more rapidly than ever, people are forced to keep up with the changing times, and geniuses are no exception. A true genius is always ahead of his time. But how far ahead must he be? In the '70s, people communicated through the postal service and rotary phones, and Jimmy Page only needed to be one year ahead of everyone else. By the time the '90s came around, the Internet and e-mail gave people access to instant information and communication. Therefore, a genius like Billy Corgan needed to stay 10 years ahead of his time, lest he risk the embarrassment of falling in line with the general public. These days, new technology grows by the minute, and you never know when the next great discovery can advance our society by ten years overnight. As a result, it's crucial that a genius like Tom DeLonge stay a minimum of 30 years ahead of his time, otherwise Apple could put out an amazing new phone and make him look stupid.

Now, I don't want to sound arrogant, but I consider myself somewhat of a genius. I've always had the suspicion that something was wrong with me, because I couldn't grasp the logic behind so much of what was going on in the world around me. Why do people divide themselves into political parties instead of working together toward common goals? Why are so many people angry at their lives, when it's often their negative attitude that keeps them down in the first place? Why do people think "Two and a Half Men" is a good show, when it clearly sucks? Questions like these kept me awake at night. I thought it was because I didn't understand the common person. Well, it turns out the common person doesn't understand me.

Why? Because I am 110 years ahead of my time. That's right, I'm so far ahead of my time that I consider Tom DeLonge and Billy Corgan to be way behind. In fact, I frequently call up Corgan and ask him if he remembered to wear his "special helmet and shoes," because by my standards, he's mentally challenged. It's really hard for me to explain my genius to the average person — even when I dumb things down, I'm still 35-40 years ahead of my time — but allow me to try.

In 2007, I worked as a writer for a music website. One of my most popular articles for the site was a list called "The 50 Hottest Women in Music." It wasn't my idea. My boss made me write it. My musical palette and writing ability is much too advanced to waste on such a pedestrian topic. Nevertheless I put quite a bit of time and effort into compiling the list. After it was published, a number of complaints were directed my way via e-mail, in the comments thread, and in write-ups on competing music websites. The number one complaint was that the list objectified women. What people didn't understand is that I wasn't objectifying anyone. Quite the opposite, in fact; I had identified an emerging trend of reverse beauty-based discrimination, and I was already working towards stopping it. Sure, everyone knows that beauty doesn't equal talent, but at the time I had noticed an underlying belief amongst the public that beautiful people can't be talented. Just because someone is attractive, does that mean they are unable to possess musical ability? It sounds ridiculous, but that somehow became a prevalent thought in this country. That's ultimately why I made the list. It was an undercover operation to prove that music fans were biased against the beautiful, and it worked perfectly. Of course, no one will understand this for about 58 years. One day, you'll see.

On another occasion, I wrote about a band called the Plain White T's and their hit song, "Hey There Delilah." I explained the story behind the song — one man's ode to a woman he barely knew — and called the band's singer a stalker. Many people were upset by that comment. But what they didn't realize is that I was giving the singer a compliment. You see, with Facebook, Twitter, and various other voyeuristic websites taking over the world, it's clear that stalking is quickly becoming a coveted talent rather than a creepy behavior. Have you ever heard a group of girls talking about a guy they met the night before, and one of the girls was bragging about how she was able to locate the guy online and find out his favorite movies and whether or not he wants children one day? Happens all the time. Imagine what things will be like in a few decades, when technological advancements allow you to see into someone's bedroom from outer space, without ever leaving your couch. Stalking will soon be a widely-desired skill, with the best stalkers getting into the best colleges and receiving the best job offers. In other words, I wasn't making fun of the Plain White T's. I was calling their singer a talented guy. Sadly, no one will grasp this concept for approximately 76 years.

And while we're on this topic, just the other day, my roommate said hello to me, and I immediately kicked him in the balls. Now, some people might say that kicking your roommate in the balls for no apparent reason is a total dick move, but what they don't understand is, I DID have a reason. The latest scientific studies have proven that humans consume an insufficient amount of oxygen, primarily due to unhealthy and unkempt homes, workplaces, buses, trains, airplanes, etc. By kicking my roommate in the balls, I caused him to gasp for air, thus increasing his oxygen intake, and in the long term, saving his life. It's too bad he won't appreciate my gesture for at least 93 years. One day he'll find me in heaven and thank me, though.

It's not easy being a genius. You put in hours and hours

of work to achieve perfection, and go out of your way to try and improve society. Yet much of your finest work is still misunderstood by the general public. Sometimes it gets frustrating, and you wonder why people can't comprehend the world on the same level that you do. Alas, I've become accustomed to this life of solitude, and I rest easy knowing that in 110 years from now, the world will finally understand my genius.

Unfortunately, you'll all be long dead by then. But three generations from now... Those guys will totally get it.

28
The Meaning of Life, Part IV

They say life is a rollercoaster.

But actually, life isn't anything like a rollercoaster. In fact, it's the exact opposite of a rollercoaster.

Life has its ups and downs. A rollercoaster also has its ups and downs, hence the comparison. But in life, the ups are great and the downs are awful. On a rollercoaster, the downs are the best part. The ups pretty much suck. During the ups, you sit in the cart with that steel bar digging into your stomach. Usually you've just eaten a bunch of fried dough and you feel like you're about to vomit 100 feet downward onto an L.A. Raiders hat that fell off some kid in the early '90s. You listen to the rollercoaster's track make that ch-ch-ch-ch-ch noise like a sample from the worst M.I.A. song ever and all you can think is, "when the hell are we going to get to the downhill part?" When you finally make it to the down, that's when the excitement kicks in and you experience true exhilaration. You throw your hands up in the air and live completely in the moment. If life was truly a rollercoaster, you'd be annoyed at the birth of your children, and you'd be fucking psyched when you got diagnosed with cancer. Also, when your life gets "flipped upside down," that's terrible. Usually it means you've had some sort of Don Draper-esque meltdown, your wife has left you, and you've just wrapped your Toyota Corolla around a streetlight with a blood alcohol content of 0.25. But being flipped upside down on a rollercoaster, well that's fantastic. You're laughing, and the rollercoaster camera is taking a picture while you and your friend make the shocker hand symbol at the person in front of you. It's great. Oh, and try taking someone's picture in real life without warning and put it on display for a bunch of cotton-candy-eating rednecks. They won't pay you $15 for an 8" x 11" print. They just kick your ass.

No, life is not like a rollercoaster at all. Life is more like the Pirate Ship. You know that ride? It's the one where a huge metal boat swings around in a circle and flips you upside down. It changes speeds on you constantly and jerks you around awkwardly. Half the time you're exhilarated, and the other half of the time you feel like you're about to puke. When you're back on the ground, you can't walk straight and you're left wondering why you had to pay so much money for something that made you feel nauseous the entire time. But you did it. You didn't sit on a bench and stuff yourself with caramel corn while your friends were having fun. You got in line, took your seat, let a carnie strap you in, and you rode the shit out of that thing. And that's the important part.

29
9 Good Things About 9/11

This year marks the 10th anniversary of 9/11, a landmark day in American history.

9/11 is the worst thing to ever happen to our country. However, there were a few small bright spots amongst the massive dark clouds. We're a country that believes in hope, so whenever we reflect on the tragedy, I think it's important to remember that a few positives did come out of 9/11. Such as...

Our country started taking defense seriously

Before 9/11 you could sail a ship made of dynamite into any U.S. port and have 30 terrorists walk off carrying warheads and firing AK-47s in the air while screaming in tongues, and no one would notice or care. Our ports were looser than a Hoboken girl on St. Patrick's Day. After 9/11 we wised up and locked things down. We started looking after our bridges and tunnels, much to the delight of guidos from New Jersey who wanted to go clubbing in Manhattan on Saturday nights and totally couldn't hook up cause "that bitch was ice cold." We tightened airport security and gave "random" searches to every suspicious-looking person (tough break, foreigners!). You can never be 100% safe but we're better off than we were.

Hilarious country songs

Alan Jackson's "Where Were You" is hands down the funniest song in the history of country music. It would probably be the funniest song ever if not for "Popular" by Nada Surf. Aside from the fact that he's exploiting a national tragedy to get a hit song, which is funny in a "you're a terrible person" sort of way, it's also some of the worst lyrics ever written. The song won a bunch of accolades and received tons of airplay, but to quote *Zoolander*, I feel like I'm taking crazy pills, because the song sucks and the lyrics don't make me feel patriotic or sympathetic in any way. The dude says in the chorus that he doesn't know the difference between Iraq and Iran! I learned that shit in 2nd grade. In the midst of the worst tragedy ever, apparently Alan Jackson's internal struggle was over whether to buy a gun or watch "I Love Lucy" reruns. And of course there was Toby Keith threatening to put a boot up terrorist's asses, which... well... honestly Toby, that's going to be worse for you than it is for them.

Boost for miniature American Flag industry

Many businesses suffered after 9/11, but the industry that makes those little flags you put on the antenna of your car was not one of them. Those things were everywhere. Some call it the golden age of miniature American Flag making. The yellow ribbon magnet industry was booming as well.

MTV played videos

No one wanted to do anything in the days following 9/11, which was understandable, but still, it made things pretty boring. Like everyone, I watched the news and was fixated on "The 9/11 Movie" for a couple of days. Eventually, you couldn't watch anymore. It was too depressing, plus they had shown every possible video clip and discussed every piece of information ad nauseum by that point. Everyone needed a change of pace. Fortunately, MTV decided to be cool and show old music videos for about 2 weeks following 9/11. I got to see classics like Soundgarden and Nirvana, along with all kinds of rare stuff like Temple of the Dog and King Missile. Pretty much all I did in the week following 9/11 was skip class, watch MTV, and drink heavily. I mean, if I did the same thing in March of 2001, that would have been one of the best weeks of my life. MTV also made U2's "Walk On" the unofficial anthem for 9/11. "Walk On" was the best song off U2's *All That You Can't Leave Behind* album, but it had never gotten the publicity it deserved because of other hits like "Elevation." In addition, MTV helped promote Bruce Springsteen's "The Rising," an inspiring tune and one of my favorites by The Boss. This kind of stuff is obviously minor in the grand scheme of things, but don't be fooled, little things like this do help people feel better during times of tragedy.

Acceptable to hate the Middle East

Let's be honest, no one likes the Middle East. There are some good people there but the region as a whole sucks. They're crazy conservative and they're always fighting over piles of dirt. It's called tolerance because we tolerate their asses, even though we all think they're annoying. In the late '90s/early '00s, our country had gotten so PC it was ridiculous. Unless you thought the world was a paradise made of rainbows and butterflies where everyone should hold hands and sing "Kumbaya," you were a terrible person. Then Drew Carey went on TV and called Arabs "towelheads" and Bill Maher rose to prominence with some non-PC remarks and the rest of the world followed suit and started saying what they really felt. I'm not advocating prejudice or stereotypes against any one group, I'm just saying that people should be free to express themselves and not have to worry about sugar-coating everything, and that we should build a giant bubble-dome over the entire Middle East and let the people there fight each other until they're all dead, then turn the region into a spring break resort. That's all I'm saying.

Ridiculously comical fear mongering

I was in college in Poughkeepsie, New York during 9/11. My school was very liberal. In my first post-9/11 class, one of my professors said that we needed to be careful, because the terrorists could strike anywhere next, EVEN US!!! Everyone in the class nodded in agreement, except me and my one friend, who gave each other a "you have to be kidding" glance. Sure, terrorists could strike Poughkeepsie. And a football team can start off a game with a quadruple-reverse flee-flicker halfback option pass. That doesn't mean it's going to happen. Fear mongering was at an all-time high after 9/11, and people thought every U.S. city was a potential target. But in reality, not every city was in danger. And that's one of the good things about 9/11. It finally gave people a reason to appreciate living in Poughkeepsie.

Hilarious catchphrases

I still can't figure out if "These Colors Don't Run" refers to the U.S.'s policy of standing up to terrorism, or if it's a reference to laundry. We may never know.

Respect for NYPD & FDNY

I like cops just slightly more than Ice Cube does, but the NYPD are the real deal. While suburban police are ticketing people for rolling through stop signs and breaking up high school parties, members of the NYPD are putting their lives at risk every day to stop real crimes and make New York the greatest city on Earth. The fact that New York has 7 million people in such a tiny area, and is still one of the safest major cities in the country, is a true testament to the fine work of the NYPD. And in my experience, no police force is better at keeping order while not harassing or trying to intimidate citizens. The FDNY is exceptional as well. Kudos to both of them.

The way people finally came together

I think that people act poorly when they are unable to experience, in a very direct and immediate manner, the negative consequences of their actions. That's why people are so much more vindictive online, where everything is anonymous, or why rich businessmen, who are allowed to get away with anything, often commit the worst acts. Meanwhile, people who live in a more interactive society, like a small Midwestern town for example, are much nicer. They know they'll be held accountable for their actions, and they want to maintain a good reputation amongst their neighbors and friends. After 9/11, the entire country became a small town community. We realized that we were all in this together. Everyone was nice. Everyone was patient. We all cared about each other and worked with each other and did what we could to help one another. We loved each other. Our old me-first way of thinking disappeared. Everything changed. The worst tragedy in our country's history brought out the best in its citizens.

At least it did for like a month, until we all reverted back to our old ways and started shoving old ladies out of the way to get into the Old Country Buffet before 5PM so we could pay the lunchtime rate. Hey, I'm sorry, but fuck that bitch, I was here first.

Never forget.

30
Solving the World's Problems With Rap Lyrics: Partisan Politics

"Politicians Be Crazy" (Democracy Remix)
by Yung Teezy

We got a problem in this country and it's only gettin' worse
Ain't talkin' bout baby mamas or n****s snatchin' purses
I'm referin' to the problem of extremist politicians
They all be goin' crazy and be actin' like bitches
See we used to have a portion of this country in the middle
But that's been fading away, little by little
Nowadays to get attention, you gotta go big
So we be sayin' crazy shit, we be livin' on the fringe
We be postin' Facebook status, putting pictures on Twitter
I released a sex tape where I was fuckin' my sister
Just to get a little press, we go to crazy lengths
We once was mild-mannered, now we act like Tyra Banks
And the politicians follow cause they wanna win our votes
So they say that gay marriage is like humans fuckin' goats
We think that they's stupid, but politicians is smart
They took our wild antics and they made it to an art

They say crazy shit and they get lots of press
Then they get into office and make our country a mess

I said UGHHH, politicians be crazy
UGHHH, politicians be crazy

Once upon a time back in ninety-three
My doctor told me I was sick with HIV
I'd been fuckin' 9 bitches but didn't want them all dead
So I cut back to fuckin' 5 bitches instead
See it's all about restraint and compromise
Politicians understand this but they still be tellin' lies
They don't care about our country, the Constitution, or their sinning
It's all about fame, cash, bitches, and winning
Now the solution to every problem is always somewhere in the middle
Between the right and the left, between the big and the little
Compromise is the cornerstone of this great nation
But you'll find more reason on "Real Housewives" than the C-SPAN station
The Senate creates problems, then they dump 'em on ya
Like when I dump Hennessey on my bitch LaTonya
Congress don't give a fuck about solvin' problems that's real
They want speaking arrangements and fat book deals
Politicians' actions make you want to scream
Like when rappers purposefully mispronounce words just to change the rhyme scheme
Whoops, sorry, I meant the rhyme skem
So fuck politicians, it's us against them!
You wanna make their impact on this world the softest?
Then stop votin' crazy mothafuckas into office!

I said UGHHH, politicians be crazy
UGHHH, politicians be crazy

Yeah yeah you know what I'm saying don't vote no republican don't vote no democrat just vote yo' heart and you can't go wrong and all I wanna say is Calvin Coolidge had some good ideas mothafuckas FEEL ME!!

31
Spoiler Alert

Bruce Willis was dead the entire time.

Jerry, George, Elaine, and Kramer are sent to prison for a year.

The chick from *The Crying Game* is really a man.

Charleton Heston was on Earth all along.

Rosebud was the name of his sled.

Clint Eastwood kills Hilary Swank.

After 10 years of acting like a bitch, Ross runs to the airport to profess his love for Rachel.

Kevin Spacey is Kaiser Soze.

On the 3rd day, Jesus rises from the dead.

The scene cuts to black and ten million people think they just sat on the remote.

Soylent Green is made out of people. PEOPLE!!!!

Matthew Fox was in purgatory. That's why his beard never grew.

Your uncle is gay. That's why he was never married.

Brad Pitt is Edward Norton.

Finkle is Einhorn.

Darth Vader is Luke's father.

Santa Claus is your dad, the Tooth Fairy is your mom, and the only Easter Bunny is made of chocolate.

Maggie shot Mr. Burns.

It was all a dream.

And when you die, that's the end of the story. You don't turn into Brad Pitt. You don't go to an island with a smoke monster. You don't get to haunt your ex-wife or talk to an 8-year old boy. You don't reunite with Jennifer Aniston or anyone else you're in love with. You just disappear like Kaiser Soze and are never seen again.

So instead of sitting around waiting for the credits, maybe you're better off spending your time doing something more productive. You can go out and help others, and you'll leave behind mourners whose lives you affected in a meaningful way, and who are so upset over your death that they cry as if they just found out their girlfriend has a cock. You can raise a child, bless him with all of your wisdom, help him avoid some of your mistakes, and teach him how to experience the kind of zest for life that Citizen Kane had when he was sledding. You can leave behind friends and family who relish the memories of all the great times you spent together, even after your life has ambiguously cut to black. You can do something that makes a difference and changes the world in way that's better, and hopefully doesn't involve monkeys taking over. Your attitude and your actions can influence others for generations, and when that happens, your story is never really over. Because people will still be quoting the scene long after the movie has ended.

But if you're watching movies all day, waiting for some surprise twist ending, all you'll probably leave behind is a giant box of DVDs.

P.S.

Snape kills Dumbledore. Fags.

32
The Silver Rule

My old company used to build websites, and as a result, we were always considering ideas for new sites. These ideas included everything from an "American Idol" style site where people voted over the most inane topics ever, to a site called "Hit in the Crotch" that would feature a multitude of articles with in-depth sociological analyses and thought-provoking philosophical questions, all of which would somehow relate back to getting hit in the crotch. And then each article would end with a video of someone getting hit in the crotch. That was my favorite idea.

Another idea I used to joke about constantly was creating a celebrity gossip site where I would write a few posts a day, just riffing on recent celebrity news. Except, there was a catch. I would pretend to be a girl, and write under a sorori-tastic name like "Ashley Stevens" or something. Every post would include my/Ashley's opinion on the story, and that opinion would always be the most entitled, bratty, stuck-up, inconsiderate, annoying rich white girl talk you could imagine. Imagine those stuck-up bitches from "Super Sweet 16," except 1,000 times worse. Ashley would truly be the worst human being ever. Say an actress was diagnosed with cancer. I would spend the whole post talking about how it's OK because she wasn't that cute anyway, and then go off on a tangent about how the guy I'm seeing was texting too much and it was annoying, so Christina Applegate and her cancer can shut up because I've got my own problems. Then be like,

"Whatever Christina, you gave us *Don't Tell Mom The Babysitter's Dead*, you got cancer, now we're even!! Lol!!!"

Of course this idea was shot down immediately.

Don't get me wrong, I understand a company not wanting to sponsor a site where I'm pretending to be the most awful girl on the planet. You can't form an effective business plan around me making fun of ugly people and comparing breaking a Prada shoe to the Armenian Genocide, which I would definitely do on day 1. But what was annoying is that someone told me the idea would never work, not because of the content itself, but because people would eventually find out that Ashley was a guy named Tom, and the resulting backlash would destroy us. In essence I was told that misrepresenting myself as a female would be a much worse crime than belittling someone's struggle with cancer.

Why is that?

I saw *The Blair Witch Project* the day it came out and thought it was pretty decent. The next day I found out it was fake and I've thought it sucked ever since. Admittedly most people knew it was fake going in, but I guess I didn't follow movie news that week. I'm from Upstate New York so I was probably busy shooting my friends with a pellet gun from a pickup truck while listening to Buckcherry, or some shit like that. The point is, the loss of authenticity changed everything. You see the same thing with music. People love a band, but then the band writes a hit song that sounds a little different than their old stuff, and the crowd turns against them. That "Million Little Pieces" book was a best seller and inspired people across the nation, but then it was discovered he was making stuff up and all of a sudden it's the worst book ever.

There are many other examples, but the lesson is clear. We demand a certain level of authenticity and morality from our public figures. You can create the greatest work of art in history, but if you sell it to people in a misrepresentative fashion, they'll hate you forever. You can be a star athlete who wins championships, but if you don't follow a certain moral code, you're a failure. You can be a successful actress who saves third-world children, but if we don't approve of your off-screen relationships, nothing else matters.

The ironic thing is that we're all inauthentic. I've worked for large corporations, and believe me, the person I was at work was completely different from the guy I was after 5PM. I would spend a weekend getting hammered and having the craziest stories, but then on Monday morning it was like, "How was my weekend? Uneventful!" Unless you have a really cool job, you probably act differently during work than you do at home. We all tell our friends stuff that we have no intention of following through on. "We should definitely go hiking this Sunday morning!" We tell our girlfriends that they look good in that shirt, even though it makes them look pregnant (you know what shirt I'm talking about). We talk about hope and changing our country and making the world a better place, but how many of us do shit?

We're also hypocritical, and our morality is suspect. When I was a child I used to complain about athletes leaving their teams to make more money in another city. They have no loyalty, I used to whine. Now that I'm in the workforce myself, I will happily ditch my company for a $10,000 raise. I wouldn't even think twice about it. Fuck 'em. It's my life and I need to get paid. The company has no loyalty to me, so why should I be loyal to them? Being employed has forced me to change my opinion on athletes, musicians, and other celebrities "selling out." I finally understand. Whether you play for the New York Giants or work at McDonald's, you shouldn't sacrifice your own career prospects to appease others.

If there's one thing I want you to take away from this book, it's that you should make inappropriate jokes publicly and as often as possible. But if there's a second thing to take away, it's that I'm kidding when I make fun of Dave Matthews or Bono or any other celebrity mentioned in a previous or upcoming chapter. I don't harbor any resentment or animosity towards any famous person, because I've lived long enough to know that they're not any different than you or me. We're all human beings with similar desires and goals. The world is one big nightclub, and each of us is just a douchebag wearing a Bluetooth and sunglasses indoors, trying to get into the VIP lounge.

In grade school, we learned about the Golden Rule. It says, "Do unto others as you would have them do unto you."

Well, in this Internet era, I'd like to propose a Silver Rule. "Don't expect from others what you wouldn't do yourself."

It's easy to criticize the actions of others when no one is paying attention to anything you do. We act piously about an athlete who goes after the money, but chances are you would do the same thing given the opportunity. We call Angelina Jolie a home wrecker to mask the fact that she's out saving the third world while we're sitting on our asses watching "Dancing With the Stars." We go on comment boards to criticize journalists for being biased, when we're too cowardly to even use our real names.

Instead of waiting for famous people to change, I think it's time we dropped our own pretenses instead. What would happen if we started taking things at face value instead of projecting our fantasies and morals onto others? What would happen if we held ourselves to the same standards that we hold actors, athletes, and rock bands?

Oh, you're waiting for an answer? I don't fuckin' know. Figure it out yourself, you lazy bastard. I just wrote this whole thing so I could slip in the cancer line without seeming like a total dick. Coming up next chapter, it's the meaning of life and AIDS jokes!!

33
The Meaning of Life, Part V

Forrest Gump once said that life is like a box of chocolates.

Well, that dude was retarded.

You see, life is more like a hot dog.

A hot dog is made of some disgusting things. Yet it tastes great. It doesn't matter what's inside it, because the end product is good.

The same could be said of life. There are some shitty parts, but when it all comes down to it, life is pretty great. Oh sure it can be overpriced and dangerous and eventually kill you from low doses of rat poison, but you've got to be a pretty cynical asshole not to enjoy the process of devouring it.

Don't worry about the details. Don't sweat the small stuff. Don't try to rinse off the dirty hot dog water because it ain't going anywhere. So what if you have to drive 45 minutes each way to get to your job? You're doing something you enjoy and you're getting paid reasonably well. Your girlfriend was once gang-banged by a bunch of 350 pound black guys, but now she's with you, and you love her. A hot dog was once a strip of boot leather, a pig urethra, and a shoelace. But now it's a hot dog and it tastes fucking delicious.

Listen, hot dogs aren't good for you, but you're not going to drop dead from one either. You're not eating a bun full of AIDS or a firecracker. It's just a hot dog, so enjoy it. Don't enjoy 500 of them, but for God's sake, have one. Don't freak out about where it's been or what it could do to your insides or whether you'll gain .5 pounds. Why do we try to ruin our own lives, to crush our own enjoyment? Whenever there's something good, we have to pick out the one bad part. If we have a chance at a better job, we worry about the additional commute time. If we have a beautiful girl, we worry about who she's been with. Whenever a tasty hot dog is there for devouring, we talk about how it's made of rat entrails and talk ourselves out of it. Shut up and enjoy life. Take the job. Marry the girl. Eat the motherfuckin' hot dog.

34
'I Knew I Had Hit Rock Bottom'

Hello boys and girls. I know this book has been a lot of fun and games so far, but now I'd like to talk to you about an experience that changed my life. This is the story of how I hit rock bottom, and how I pulled myself up from those depths to achieve a fulfilling and satisfying life. I am sharing this story not because I want to brag or put myself on a pedestal, but rather as inspiration for any of you who feel your life is not as great or meaningful as it should be.

I grew up Catholic, going to church every Sunday morning. Both of my parents were pretty heavy into religion, and each week my family would pile into the minivan and head off to hear a sermon about the miraculous workings of Jesus Christ. I would sit there for an hour, listening to the priest talk about God and his wonderful creations.

It started off innocently enough, just a way to spend time with my family each week.

But as habits tend to do, it slowly spiraled out of control.

It was pretty inconspicuous at first, just a weekly sermon and maybe a communion here or there. Oh sure, I knew I hadn't done my First Communion yet, and I shouldn't be accepting the sacrament, but I figured, "what's the big deal, it's just a piece of bread." Soon I was taking communion every week. And that's not all.

I began attending Sunday School sessions in addition to the usual sermon. As the years went on, things got worse, and I found myself skipping out on school to go to church and attend religious retreats. My grades slipped as I gave more and more of my time and attention to God. A former straight-A student, I was nearly flunking social studies. My best subject. At least three times a day, I would lock myself in my room and pray. I can vividly remember blasting *The Chronic* in order to make my parents think I was in there listening to gangsta rap, but really, I was in there praying. Praying for relatives, praying for myself, praying for world peace, praying for any and everything I could think of. It eventually got so bad, I couldn't even make it through a family dinner or a game of *Super Mario 3* without praying. I could beat *Mario 3* with my eyes closed, and yet, I still prayed every game.

That's when I realized that I had become a full-blown God addict.

As a child, you often don't fully understand the extent or consequences of your actions. Religion is such a seductive thing for a young man, and in hindsight it's easy to see how I got hooked. There was the sacrament, oh that sweet, sweet body of Christ. The communion wine was plentiful and always flowing. Sunday School was a brothel of attractive pre-teens in gorgeous sundresses. It was such a natural high, what young man could resist? Not me, that's for sure.

Well, old habits die hard, and soon I had completely lost control of my life. I knew I had hit rock bottom, when at the age of 17, I found myself curled up on the bathroom floor of my studio apartment, crying hysterically to only myself and the rats that infested my hellish abode. You see, my parents had kicked me out of the house when they caught me praying instead of taking out the trash, a task that I had been assigned on the "Chore Board" (a whiteboard magnetically attached to our refrigerator). To make ends meet, I began selling bootleg Bibles door-to-door in one of the roughest neighborhoods in town. I knew it was dangerous, but I foolishly believed that God would protect me from the inhabitants of the local crack houses. One day, while peddling Good Books, a stray bullet from a drive-by hit me in the shoulder. There was blood everywhere. I ran back to my apartment, my shirt soaked through like a dark red rag. I grabbed a bottle of Hawaiian Punch that I had been trying to ferment into sacramental wine and splashed it all over the affected area. Nothing. Defeated, I grabbed a slice of 3-week old Wonderbread, the only food in the house. I placed the bread in a large spoon, and held a lighter underneath the spoon, attempting to create my own communion. In my demented mind, I thought it was the only chance for survival. I had successfully made this type of knockoff communion before, and although it wasn't as good as the real thing, it was much cheaper and I was still able to get high if I took just a little more. Unfortunately, this particular loaf of Wonderbread was infested with mold, and the combination of moldy low-grade communion and severe blood loss sent me into a coma. Before slipping away, I grabbed the phone and tried to call for help, but sadly my phone had been shut off because I gave away all my money toward tithing and didn't even have enough to pay the bill.

As I lay there, completely O.D.ed on God, I had what most people refer to as a near-death experience. I walked down a white tunnel, and at the end I saw a giant glass with ice cubes and a strange brownish colored liquid in it. I didn't know what it meant at the time, but as it turned out, this vision would prove to be a foreshadowing of the moment that forever changed my life.

I finally came to after what seemed like an eternity. I looked at my clock and saw that I had been unconscious for twenty minutes. Later I would discover that I had been clinically dead for eight of those minutes. I got up and walked down the street to Jeremy's house. Jeremy was my one and only friend. He was the only person that didn't abandon me during my downward spiral into religion. Unless you've been there, you probably wouldn't understand, but take it from me: When you get that deep into God, you lose a lot of friends. At first people say they want to help, but soon you notice that everyone is distancing themselves from you. It's like I've said ever since, "When you're taking 12 communions a day, you find out who your real friends are."

When I reached Jeremy's house, I tried to explain what happened, but I didn't have the energy to get the words out. He took one look at my bullet wound and began to pour a strange liquid on it. It burned at first, but shortly afterwards I began to feel better. He then poured the same liquid in a glass and told me to drink it. Wouldn't you know it, within an hour I felt like nothing had happened. I had this feeling of floating on air. My head felt lighter, ugly women suddenly appeared attractive, and I was filled with a feeling of love for everyone around (except for this one guy, who was a fuckin' dick and I wanted to kick his ass).

Jeremy eventually took me to the hospital. When I

regained consciousness after the bullet-removal surgery, I woke up to see Jeremy's smiling face. He grabbed me, walked me to his car, and drove back to his place. He sat me in the living room and proclaimed, "Wait here while I get you a drink." I will remember this moment as long as I live, because it was this moment that changed my life forever. When Jeremy returned, he was holding a glass filled with ice and a strange brownish colored liquid. It was the exact image I had seen in my near-death experience. I knew this was a sign. I accepted the glass, took a giant swig, and asked Jeremy, "What is this magical liquid you bring before me?"

He looked at me, gave a half-smile, and said:

"That, my friend, is Bacardi and Coke."

I was in shock. This liquid that eased my pain, that blurred my vision, that made the average-looking chick next door to Jeremy appear very do-able… this is what saved my life?

Don't get me wrong. I had heard of Bacardi before. Oh, I had even tried it a couple times, at parties in the woods or at some kid's house whose parents were out of town. But I had never fully *embraced the idea* of Bacardi before. That's when I realized there was a massive void in my life that could be filled only by delicious alcohol. All my life, what I had been searching for was right in front of me, up a couple feet and a little to the right, in the kitchen cabinet where my father kept his alcohol stash. For years I had tried to fill that void with things like God and prayer, but I was only living a lie. In actuality I was just hiding from what I really wanted: Booze.

That day, I vowed to change my life around. I began drinking every single day, going to bars as often as possible. I got drunk frequently, met tons of new people, had lots of fun, and hooked up with a bunch of chicks. Life was truly amazing. I was doing it. I was living the dream. It was a life I never could've imagined just a few years back, when I was lying to my family and holding up Bishops at gunpoint just to steal a little sacrament so I could get high. Sure, it was a tough transition. I won't lie, I thought about God a lot at first, but eventually I was able to banish those thoughts, to the point where I could go months without even wanting a communion, instead focusing all my attention toward alcohol and partying. As my liver's capacity to function properly dissolved, so did my desire to pray. It took a lot of effort on my part, as I had to leave my old ways completely behind and commit to a life of getting plastered on rum n' cokes. I had to find new people to hang out with, as I couldn't be around the same God-pushing enablers that had led me down my original destructive path. I had to start a brand new life. But I did it, and now, I wake up every single day and thank the Bacardi Corporation for my newfound, meaningful existence. Without their succulent light rum and delectable flavors, especially Limon, I might not be here today. Hell, I *probably* wouldn't be here today.

The point, kids, is that there's always time to get back your life. A few short years ago, I was an absolute train wreck and I wouldn't have given myself much chance of living past 21. Unfortunately it took me hitting rock bottom before I realized the error of my ways. But I made a change, and now here I am. Not just alive, but living well. And I owe it all to alcohol.

No matter how bad things get, no matter how bleak the

future may appear, always remember: It's never too late to turn things around.

If any of you are trying to change your life, hopefully this story has inspired you, and I wish you the best of luck in your endeavor. Before I go, I just want to thank my lord and savior, Carolina Bacardi. In the name of the father, son, and the holy mojito.

35
The Solution to All of the World's Problems

Gay Marriage

Let them get married. Hey, we all hate Cher's music and nobody likes seeing gay guys act all peppy all the time. It makes us feel like we're not living our own lives to the fullest. But to prevent gay people from getting married is to deny them the same rights as everyone else, which is discrimination of the highest form and goes against everything that the Constitution of the United States stands for. There is no defense for outlawing gay marriage, save for homophobic bigotry or religious-based propaganda, neither of which should be deemed an acceptable reason for anything. Gay couples may not be society's "ideal" situation, but if that's true then neither are single parents, interracial couples, alcoholics, asshole fathers, or any number of other combinations that make up ¾ of the families in America. The people who are against gay marriage are simply against gay people and will use any excuse necessary to rationalize their hatred of homosexuals. In 50 years we'll look back on gay rights in the 2000s decade the same way we look back at civil rights and women's rights in the 1960s. Although progress is always slow, equality is inevitable. Those who strive for progress always win. Those who get in the way of progress not only fail, but are remembered as the ultimate dicks of history. So make a choice. You can support gay marriage, or you be this generation's version of the people who turned fire hoses on black people in Alabama. It's your choice. Do the right thing. Plus, turning your fire hose on the gays... well dude, that's pretty damn gay.

The Internet & The End of Privacy

This is a bullshit problem. The only problem here is that we've somehow tricked ourselves into believing that we ever had privacy in the first place. I know that Amy Smith blew Mark Reesing under the bleachers in 9th grade, and I never said more than 3 words to either of them. Everyone knows everything about everyone already. Word of mouth travels just as fast as a DSL line. Sure, it's annoying to think that drunken pictures of you are floating around on Facebook, but the same thing is happening to 99% of the world. So it's a level playing field. The corporate world will eventually catch up to the times and start overlooking minor offenses like party photos, or they won't have any employees in 10 years. We're headed towards a more lax corporate environment. You can mark that down. If you're truly that concerned about online privacy, there's a simple solution. Don't use the internet. For normal people, there's another solution. You can let the Internet embarrass you, or you can use it as a tool to display your talents, achievements, and creativity. Make a website. Create a LinkedIn profile. Post your resume online. Write an article for a local newspaper. There are a million ways to get good publicity online and overshadow any photos of you funneling a beer. And for the record, if someone has nothing embarrassing online, it means they've probably lived a boring and unfulfilling life. So let people post pictures or talk about you online. The day you have real privacy is the day no one gives a fuck about you.

War

War is an inevitable part of humanity, unfortunately. We're all dicks. However, do we really need to send humans into battle? Where are the robot soldiers? We have robots that vacuum our rug, but we can't develop a robot soldier? Most of America's enemies are rebels armed only with a steak knife and a Molotov cocktail. Do we really need humans to take them down? Let's get our best and brightest to stop working on smartphone apps and start creating a robot-based defense system. That way we can continue our imperialism of the world without putting our brave soldiers at risk. Yeah, you heard me, Iran! Americabot 3000 is coming to fuck you up!

Drugs

Listen up, kids. Drugs are awful. They slowly destroy your body both inside and out, making you look old and weathered, and withering away your internal organs to the point of no return. Meanwhile, they mess up your brain's ability to make rational decisions, deteriorating your judgment, until one day, in your demented mind, you actually believe that an overdose wouldn't be that bad of an option. That's why you should avoid drugs and stick to hardcore binge drinking. Not only does alcohol taste great, but it makes you really happy and causes members of the opposite sex to find you irresistible. And there are no side effects whatsoever. It's like that PSA from the 1980s… "When you drink booze, you can't lose!" Or something like that.

Abortion

A human embryo is compositionally similar to the embryos of several other species, including tadpoles. Therefore it's logical to surmise that aborting a baby in the embryonic stage is the same as ending the life of a frog. I strongly believe in consistency. Therefore as I see it we have two options. Our first choice is to continue with our current pro-choice laws, allow women to make their own decisions regarding their bodies, ignore hypocritical moralists and their intrusive and judgmental attitudes, and punish asshole vigilantes who try to take matters into their own hands by attacking abortion doctors. Or we can make abortion AND frog murder illegal. Personally I prefer the latter. It may seem intense to send a 2nd grade class to jail for 10 years for dissecting a frog, but remember, that frog was an innocent victim who could've grown up to be President of the United States, so as far as I'm concerned those kids can burn in hell. God will judge you for your sins, little Billy!! Dissection is murder!!!

Obesity

Stop eating.

The Death Penalty

Like many of the problems facing our country today, the death penalty is not a simple issue. Politicians and stupid people love to discuss complicated matters as if they had black-and-white answers, but in reality there are valid arguments both for and against the death penalty. In my opinion, the death penalty is an issue that must be decided on a case-by-case basis. While I hate to support the killing of any human being, there are certainly people who don't deserve to be alive. When a criminal commits an incredibly heinous act like murder or rape, he is backing out of an understood social contract and thus giving up his right to continue living. Of course we have a judicial system that must make the difficult choice of whether or not to put a convicted criminal to death, and I believe that the American people are discerning enough to get this decision right in 99.99% of cases. Just as any criminal is "innocent until proven guilty," the sentence for convicted murderers should be life in prison unless it can be proven overwhelmingly that the death penalty is well-deserved. Then, after the criminal is allowed no more than two failed appeals, they should promptly be put to death in the most appropriate way possible, preferably by jamming a sharpened broomstick up their rectum until they bleed out.

Childhood Obesity

Stop letting your kids eat.

Poverty

The only way we're going to eliminate poverty worldwide is through a combination of charity and reduced consumption. First we need to start with reduced consumption. America is the wealthiest country in the world and we all buy a ton of things that we don't really need. We could stop going out to eat so much when a nice home-cooked meal is cheaper and healthier. We could save our money and purchase a simple, reliable 4-door sedan instead of a gas-guzzling sports car. We could stop buying enormous quantities of food and throwing out spoiled remains that we never got around to eating. We shouldn't buy a third TV when two will do just fine. We don't need to stick to just the bare necessities, but we also don't need to overindulge. Charity can't be a government mandate; it must come from within the hearts of individuals. By striking a simple balance and sticking to what's truly important, we'll be able to save ourselves an inordinate amount of money every year. It's then crucial that we recognize how blessed we were simply to be born to decent parents in the wealthiest country in the world, and in turn donate some of our savings to those less fortunate than ourselves.

I'm just kidding. Fuck those guys. If they didn't want to be poor, they shouldn't have been born in some shitty third-world country. Hahaha, enjoy the malaria, losers!

Adult Obesity

Stop eating. Exercise. Jesus Christ man, have some willpower.

Terrorism & the Middle East

This is a simple problem with a simple solution. "What?!?," you ask? The reason terrorists and so many others in the Middle East hate us is because they think we live an overindulgent, Godless lifestyle of pre-marital sex and endless mass consumption. Which is of course correct. But… they've also been brainwashed into thinking this is a bad thing. So how do we counter this propaganda? We fly a bunch of planes over the Middle East and initiate a massive airstrike. Except instead of bombs, we drop millions of Britney Spears videos. I'm talking about early Britney Spears: "Baby One More

Time," "Oops... I Did It Again," etc. All the pre-Federline stuff. Make sure there's at least 100,000 copies of the "I'm a Slave 4 U" video, the greatest video ever created. You can throw in some early Jessica Simpson too if you want. Once those sex-craved terrorists see what they're missing out on, they'll recognize that America is the greatest country on Earth and they'll change their terrorizing ways real fast. "You told me America was evil empire! But this girl, she dance with snake! In America, they have girls such as this? Allah, you have lied to me!"

Lack of Human Compassion

People need tragedy to appreciate life. When I was in high school we had a guest speaker who had lost his leg in a motocross accident. I'm sure you've seen someone like this. The guy was so enthusiastic about life! Yet the whole time he was speaking, we teenagers were daydreaming and quietly gossiping about the past weekend. We were 17, able-bodied, and had no real responsibilities, but we were miserable and all we cared about was meaningless high school gossip. Meanwhile the guest speaker was in his 30s, probably had huge piles of unpaid medical bills, and he had NO FUCKING LEG, but he had an amazing attitude. It's because he understood that he was lucky to even be alive, and he knew he couldn't let a negative attitude destroy the opportunity he had been given.

Many of us get so caught up in our day-to-day activities that we lose sight of the big picture. Few things are truly important; life, love, friendship, a sense of purpose, freedom, and basic human rights being among them. In America most of us have these things. However we incessantly complain about things like traffic or the price of milk or annoying co-workers. It's because these negatives suddenly appear in your face, while positives like friendship and your life are constant, hovering in the background. You take the good for granted and bitch about anything that's bad.

That's why I believe the government should set up a special Happiness Task Force. Members of this task force would go around and secretly kill one member of every family. They'll choose oldest or least successful member of every family; that way it's not a huge loss. They'll also make it look like an accident so surviving family members get a sense of the awesome power and randomness of the universe. Trust me, when your Grandpa Mike is found dead of auto-erotic asphyxiation at age 82, you'll think twice before whining about a traffic jam. Once the Happiness Task Force has completed its mission of quietly murdering roughly 50 million Americans, everyone who's left will start to appreciate the value of life. Plus we'll probably have less traffic with all those people gone. It's a win-win.

Declining Interest in the Catholic Church

The Catholic Church is having a difficult time attracting new members, and an even tougher time getting people to become priests. It's not surprising. I tried becoming a priest once, but I had to give it up after a year or so. I loved the religion, don't get me wrong, but I got too bogged down in the day-to-day work of the job and never got a chance to focus on the big picture. Like, I would try to formulate a scheme for covering up mass child molestation and making it look like an atheist anti-church conspiracy, but then I'd have to stop working every 45 minutes to help quiet down some boy who just got molested. It all became too much, and eventually I quit. The priesthood is nothing but red tape. You have no idea. Seriously, Catholic Church, ease up on the bureaucracy and let a brother do his job.

Greed

The other day I was looking at a picture of two Wall Street guys. They must've had a good day because both guys were giving a thumbs up while doing an awkward arm-around-the-back pseudo-hug. They were also yelling something. It appeared to be the phrase "yeah baby!" And it made me laugh, because these guys were celebrating a good day trade with the same zest most people reserve for the birth of their first child. Over the past few years, as we experienced the greatest recession in a generation, many Americans felt contempt for Wall Streeters and the greedy attitude that brought our economy to its knees. Fortunately life is a beautiful thing. Because if you're a tool, then no matter how much money you have, you're still going to look like a tool. Money can buy houses and cars and yachts and more money, but it can't buy you a personality. The greatest argument that God exists is the fact that a couple of Wall Street guys with millions of dollars can still look like total d-bags. They might have unlimited money but they'll never have my respect. Trust me, even I was living in a gutter somewhere, and out of nowhere some guy handed me a billion dollars, it still wouldn't make me act like a complete tool. Oh, I'd take the money, and I'd buy myself a yacht, and I'd hire a midget servant to pour champagne over some naked strippers as a group of supermodels fanned me and fed me grapes. But, and this I promise you, I would NEVER do an over-the-top smile combined with the awkward thumbs up and back pat while screaming "yeah baby!" Some things are more important than money, and not looking like a fucking tool is one of them.

Sloth

I don't know what sloth is. I know it's one of the seven deadly sins, because it was in that movie *Seven*, but that movie came out a long time ago and I can only remember the end. I think it has something to do with being slow or liking candy bars or something like that. Anyway, it's supposedly a big deal, but then again, gluttony is one of the seven deadly sins and I wouldn't exactly call overeating a massive priority what with poverty and war and Africa and whatnot. I'm sure if I knew what sloth was I'd have a pretty good solution for it, but I'm way too lazy to look it up, so whatever.

School Shootings

There are five kids in every high school that have the potential to go Columbine, and everyone in the school knows exactly who they are. These kids wear all black, they're smart but get bad grades due to a horrible work ethic, and they listen to whatever today's version of Marilyn Manson is. Just to clarify, I'm not saying Manson caused Columbine. I'm just saying his *one* CD did. Anyway, let's get all high school freshmen to fill out a survey ranking the top 5 Columbine-esque suspects in their school. Sort of like an AP Poll for creepy loners. I suspect we'll see a lot of overlap in every school. Have you ever seen an interview where former classmates talk about a mass murderer and say, "This is a total shock, 5 years ago he was listening to No Doubt and loved skipping down the street!" No. Weird people were always weird, and high school kids can spot a future crazed gunman better than anyone. So we take this survey and we put the highest-ranked kids on a government watch list for the next 15 years. Some critics will call this Orwellian, but I prefer to think of it as a really bad Senior Superlative.

Arrogant Celebrities

Celebrities like LeBron James and Kanye West are always getting in trouble for their arrogance and bad attitudes. What you need to understand is, these are human beings. They're known only for their musical or athletic skills, yet they have dozens of other interests. When you're a multi-dimensional person, it's extremely frustrating to deal with a public that treats you like a one-talent wonder, and sometimes your temper gets the best of you. I can totally relate. The other day I went for a job interview with an Internet marketing company. I told the hiring manager that I had vast experience in SEO, SEM, and social media marketing. She was like, "this job focuses mainly on SEM, and although you might get to do a little SEO or social media stuff here and there, SEM will make up the bulk of your workday." I screamed, "DON'T PIDGEONHOLE ME WOMAN!!!!" then grabbed a lamp off her desk and smashed it over her head before storming out. Some would say I handled the situation wrong, but I stand by my decision. I'm very passionate when it comes to search engine optimization.

Meteor Strikes

If a meteor hits the Earth, we're all fucked. Sorry.

Weight Loss

OK, so I made a few dismissive jokes about obesity earlier, but I now I'd like to share my one and only weight-loss secret. I've found that an effective way to lose weight and get in shape is when you're not able to afford food or public transportation. You starve and you have to walk everywhere, and the result is a picture-perfect lean physique. I call it the "New York City Diet." Give it a shot. It works.

Legalization of Marijuana

No one cares if marijuana is legal. It won't change anything. People who want to smoke already do, and people who don't smoke now aren't going to run out and buy a 6-foot bong if we legalize weed. That said, pro-marijuana people, can you please stop comparing marijuana to alcohol? Hey, listen, if you want to advocate for legalization, that's great, go for it. There are plenty of logical reasons for legalization, such as the tax benefits and the elimination of the failed War on Drugs. But stop fucking over us alcoholics. Every time you say that alcohol is more dangerous than marijuana, lawmakers are thinking, "Yeah, you're right, we should make drinking illegal too!" There are two things you need to know about our elected officials. They love creating useless new laws, and they hate fun. So by decreeing that alcohol is dangerous, you're not helping the pro-marijuana cause. You're only helping to write new alcohol-related legislation and take us one step closer to a world where fun is outlawed. You're escalating the War on Drugs into the War on Fun. So shut the hell up stoners, or I swear to God I'll gather every copy of *The Big Lebowski* on Earth and burn them all. I like that movie too, but I want to make it clear that I'm not fucking around.

Social Media

In the 21st century, many companies have turned to social media-based solutions in lieu of creating actual, quality products. Some people find this troubling, but those people are wrong. Social media and user-generated content is the way of the future. Why hire one "professional" to do a job when you could get input from thousands of everyday people instead? That's why I suggest we immediately take social media marketing and translate it to other aspects of life. Like movies for example. The problem with movies is, you didn't write them. I didn't write *Good Will Hunting* and therefore it sucked!! Or what about art? Andy Warhol's paintings were OK, but they'd be way better if they were painted by you! And let's not limit this idea to artistic endeavors. How about social media pilots? Pilots are annoying. They talk about what state you're flying over and ring a bell when they want you to buckle your seatbelt. How lame! With social media piloting, everyone gets a turn at the controls and the loudspeaker. You want to tell that story about the time you beat *Grand Theft Auto 3* in just twenty minutes while piloting a flight from San Francisco to Boston? You got it, buddy! And don't get me started on doctors. Why do we have to listen to one jackass spouting off with his diagnosis? You always hear about getting a "second opinion." With social media medicine, you could get thousands of opinions from people who have also been sick at some point in their life! Finally, let's ride the wave of social media into the classroom. No more stupid teachers always telling you what happened and what didn't happen. Abraham Lincoln freed the slaves? Nope, sorry, we took a poll and it turns out it was Mike Hunt. Thanks for making our country so great, Mike Hunt!

<u>Kids</u>

I am going to be the worst parent ever. Don't get me wrong, I'll love my kids very dearly, but when they ask for shit like Justin Bieber tickets, I'm going to try Ticketmaster once, find out the concert is sold out, and then tell them to shut the hell up and play with blocks like I used to when I was growing up (blatantly disregarding the fact that I grew up with Super Nintendo). This may be hypocritical, but as a long-term strategy it's going to work. You see, when I'm a father, much in the same way that Justin Timberlake brought sexy back, I'm going to bring discipline back. I'm not as marketable as J.T., but I think this will catch on. Kids these days have it too easy and it's time for parents to take back control. What's the point in spoiling your kid when they won't even remember it in ten years anyway? If I have a daughter... well, she's getting locked in the basement til she's 30, so that won't be an issue. But if I have a son, he's just going to have to learn some hard lessons, like "you can't always get what you want" and "daddy doesn't look for concert tickets because it cuts into his drinking."

Happiness is a state of mind. So when you almost kill yourself to get Justin Bieber tickets, what's next? Kids aren't really the appreciative type. They'll just expect that same kind of dedication the next time they want something. "Daddy, why can't I see *Shrek 8*? I don't care if it's sold out!!! Why won't you enter a contest and win tickets?!?!?! AAAHHHH!!!!" Then the crying starts, and you have to lock the kid in the car, and OF COURSE that's when your neighbor comes over to borrow a rake and things get really awkward.

The Ending of "The Sopranos"

I know what you're thinking: This isn't really a problem, Tom. You're an idiot. I hope you die in a rattlesnake pit. However, the debate over whether or not Tony died at the end of "The Sopranos" is a battle that has been fought ever since the show ended in 2007. Many people think that Tony was killed, and that the stirring cut to black that ended the series' 6-year run was indicative of his death. Others believe that the ending of the show signified Tony's uncertain future; that while he remained alive, he would always have to live his life in fear of retaliation, a fear possibly greater than death.

What people are forgetting is one simple fact. It's a fucking TV show. Tony didn't live or die, because he didn't exist in the first place. He was a fictional character created by a writer named David Chase. A real human in Tony Soprano's predicament would have faced two possible outcomes: Death or a life of fear. But a writer of a fictional TV show has a third option. He can purposely create an ambiguous ending in order to spark debate and make a long-lasting impression. David Chase won't clarify what happened in "The Sopranos" because he knows the legacy of the series will be tied to the uncertainty and debate over the show's conclusion. Chase revealing the meaning of the finale would be like God coming down from the sky and telling you the meaning of life. Don't you think that would take some of the intrigue away from living? "Yo dude, it's God... I got something to tell you... no, it's not about your family… to be honest family and friendship aren't really that important to me… yeah, no, actually the meaning of life is to play video games as often as possible… yeah, crazy, right… anyway I gotta run, Marilyn Monroe's getting in the hot tub."

I'll tell you what happened to Tony Soprano. Nothing. Want to know what Tony was thinking during those final moments? Nothing. Want to know whether he's dead or alive? Neither. It's fake.

Now remember at the beginning of this paragraph when you told me this wasn't a real problem and then called me an idiot and suggest I die? Technically you're right. You're kind of an asshole, but you're right. People debating the end of "The Sopranos" isn't a big deal in the grand scheme of things. However, peoples' inability to differentiate between real life and fiction has become a huge problem. "The Sopranos" ends and people argue non-stop about what happened to Tony. In our minds we know it's a fictional TV show, but we've spent so much time bonding with Tony Soprano that we want to know he's still OK when all is said and done. Similarly, actors are typecast all the time. It's not because they don't have the talent to play other roles. It's because the audiences can only accept them as one character. We've watched James Gandolfini whack so many people that we'd have a hard time believing him as, say, Santa Claus. Meanwhile, in a far off land, someone draws a cartoon of Mohammed and is murdered by a group of hardcore Muslims. Even if you're a devout follower of Mohammed, you should be able to recognize that the cartoon was only one man's portrayal. It was an opinion. It didn't DO anything. The drawing didn't leap off the page and teach Muslim children to smoke. But someone out there was unable to discern between fantasy and reality, and now a cartoonist is dead. The mental defect that allows some people to believe Tony Soprano is a real person is the same defect that allows others to go crazy and murder cartoonists. We live in a world where people are killing each other because of Facebook posts, for Christ's sake. Maybe no one died over the ending of "The Sopranos," but the way I see it, we're only ten years away from someone getting murdered over their opinion about the ending of a TV show. Oh, and we're five years away from someone being murdered over a fantasy football league.

This blurring of fantasy and reality is extremely dangerous. Listen, I think Tony Soprano lived and the cut to black was representative of a future where he would always be on edge. I believe that Pat Bateman was delusional and didn't really murder anyone. I believe that Tommy Lee Jones stopped chasing Javier Bardem and that his retirement was an expression of free will and an unwillingness to let evil or the randomness of the world control his life. I think the guy from *Memento* tricked himself into chasing a ghost because it gave his life a sense of purpose. I still don't know what the hell happened in *Inception*. I appreciate the artistic vision of those movies, but I'm not about to get into a fight with someone who has a different take on an ambiguous work of fiction. You know why? Because I'm sane. If I were mentally unbalanced, I would think that Tony Soprano was an actual person. I would believe that he actually got shot by a guy in a Members-Only jacket. I would believe that Meadow Soprano was a living, breathing girl who couldn't parallel park for shit, and that I had a chance to fuck her. I would listen to a pundit create a ridiculous caricature of our President, then show up at a rally with an uzi in order to show my displeasure with a fictionalized version of a politician. I would think that a painting about a fairy in the clouds was a direct insult to my supreme ruler and I'd try to murder the person who drew it. I would blur the lines between fiction and reality until I could no longer understand the difference between the two, and the only thing I had left to do was to argue and fight for my twisted beliefs. My sanity would have cut to black, and it definitely would not have survived.

Distracted Driving

I hate people who talk on the phone or text while driving. It's not because they swerve all over the road. It's because I can't understand who the fuck these people are talking to at 8AM. Every morning I drive to work and pass at least 25 people on the phone. I only have a 15-minute commute. I've never received a phone call before noon in my entire life, and yet each day in America there are thousands of people on the phone during rush hour traffic. They couldn't wait until they were done driving to make those calls, but furthermore, they couldn't even wait until the start of business hours. I get annoyed when people call me at work before 9:30. (Let me settle in, asshole!) Yet right now, somewhere in the world, it's 8AM, a person is dialing from the driver's seat, and there's someone on the receiving end of that call who's excited to pick up the phone. Someone is overjoyed that they get to have a conversation at 8AM. Never in my life has anyone loved me even close to that much. Not my girlfriend, not my friends, not my siblings or my parents. No one has EVER called me at 8AM, and although I'm not rude enough to call someone else at 8AM, I know that if I did, that person would definitely not pick up. That's why I hate distracted drivers. Because they make me feel unloved.

Fortunately I have a plan to stop these distracted drivers and the heartbreaking pain they cause to so many.

What do we know about distracted drivers? Well, obviously, they need to be distracted. Focusing on the road for 20 minutes at a time is too boring for these people, so their attention deficit disorder forces them to do something more entertaining, like texting. We also know another thing. People with ADD love shitty pop music. The same lack of focus that causes people to text while driving also causes them to tune into Z98's Wacky Zoo Crew in the Morning for drive-time entertainment. That's why we need to identify the shittiest pop station in every major city and secretly transmit cell phone-blocking waves over the same frequency. As distracted drivers bob their heads to the repetitive beats of a crappy new Rihanna song, we'll be sending out a signal that blocks their cell service. This will prevent distracted drivers from using their phone while on the road. Or at the very least, they'll have to start listening to better music.

Illegal Immigration

Everyone in Mexico wants to come to the United States. The United States is a land of freedom and opportunity, while Mexico is a place you go for burritos, drunken sex, and drug-related murders. I don't know why you'd be seeking out drug-related murders, but hey man, it's your life. Point being that Mexicans will always attempt to sneak into our country. Our immigration process is so lengthy and convoluted that few immigrants waste their time trying to enter the U.S. through legal methods.

Let's be honest for a second. We could reform our immigration process to make it easier for Mexicans to enter our country legally. But it won't happen. Why? Because we don't like them. Think about it. When you mention "illegal immigration," everyone's mind immediately jumps to Mexico. Illegal immigrants could come from any other country in the world. But mention the phrase and our thoughts don't exactly race to a blond-haired Swedish guy named Sven trying to hop a fence. We have nothing against immigrants. This country was founded on immigrants. We just don't like Mexicans. They steal our jobs, they don't speak English, they sell drugs, their skin color is weird, and I HATE THINGS THAT ARE DIFFERENT!!!

That's why we need a special immigration process for Mexico. Remember that show "American Gladiators?" We need to recreate the set of the show along our southern border. Any Mexican who wants to enter the U.S. will have to make it through the Assault course. The Gladiators will fire tennis balls at the Mexicans as they hide behind Mexican-themed barriers, like a broken-down Pinto or a giant plastic taco shell. If contestants/immigrants can make it to the end of the course without being shot, they'll become an official American citizen! In fact, we'll use the Texas border as the finish line. Oh, and also, instead of tennis balls, we'll shoot bullets. So you either win citizenship, or you die. That may sounds harsh but you've got to have risk to get reward. And to the Mexicans that make it across the border: Congratulations on defeating our best Gladiators, and we welcome you and your super powers to America!

Elections

If you have to pick a political party, I recommend becoming a Democrat, because no matter what happens in an election, you win. Either your candidate is elected, or a Republican takes office and you have good music for the next 4 years. I don't know what it is about conservatives but they can't write a good tune to save their lives. There's Lynyrd Skynyrd and like 2 other good Republican bands, and 80 million good Democrat bands. This is where some of you might mention country artists, but you're forgetting that you have terrible taste in music. Since all the good bands are liberal, a Republican President ensures at least four years of good solid political protest music.

The truth, however, is that you're better off not aligning with any political party, or any candidate at all for that matter. No political candidate is going to change your life. Only you can do that. An ounce of personal initiative is worth a ton of legislation. Plus, elections are so heartbreaking. They start out with a bunch of people, you get attached to one, and then your candidate loses the primary and disappears from your life forever. It's kind of like dating George Clooney. That's right, Clooney, I know your game, and if you don't call my sister back then I will NEVER buy a hybrid car.

Reality TV

America's desire to murder reality stars and watch the streets run red with the blood of the non-talented is rivaled only by the Nielsen ratings of the trashy programs we secretly and hypocritically love. Reality stars are like tampons; we can't get by without them, yet as soon as we're done with them we want to immediately throw them in the trash. Well, guess what, people, reality TV isn't going anywhere, so you can either embrace it or change the channel. I'm all for jokes, but it's sad to see people who are genuinely distraught over the existence of reality TV. Their complaints fall into two categories. First, the obvious. "Reality TV sucks." Thanks buddy, you got any other observations, maybe something about the sky being blue? Second, the lies. I've noticed a lot of people pretending they think that all reality stars are ugly. I guess it makes them feel better about themselves to not admit an untalented person might be attractive. Now, some reality stars are better-looking than others, and none are the Marilyn Monroe of our era, but when it comes down to it, many of them are attractive. That's what is so interesting to me about reality TV. Girls became famous for doing "nothing" and so some people will refuse to give them any sort of a compliment. When I hear a guy say that Kim Kardashian is ugly, all I can think is, "Congratulations, you're really a man of principle. And that principle is, you're gay."

Taxes

First we must agree that taxes are a necessary evil. Nobody is ever happy about the amount of taxes they pay. Whether they pay a dollar a year, or a million dollars a year, no one on Earth has ever said, "Man, my taxes are way too low! Someone should raise them ASAP!" Coming up with a fair tax plan is a fool's errand, because people love to complain, and taxes make the perfect topic for bitching.

With that in mind, I think I've created the most fair tax system possible.

Nobody likes trust fund babies or those who inherited a large sum of money without earning it. Still, it's unfair to tax someone at a higher percentage based solely on wealth. Let's say you raise taxes on the rich to 50%. Someone making $1 million a year would end up paying $500,000 a year in taxes. They would end up paying more than hundreds of other people combined. This hurts real entrepreneurs. People like Mark Zuckerberg and Bill Gates shouldn't have to pay enormous taxes just because they had a good idea. We're punishing our most successful citizens.

On the flip side, a flat tax doesn't work. A millionaire isn't hurt by a 35% flat tax, but an entry-level worker making $30,000 a year would end up taking home less than $20,000 after taxes. There are young professionals across the country who work 50-hour weeks and still have to eat Ramen every night. They aren't welfare queens or leeches. They are hardworking individuals who get screwed by our current tax system. A flat tax would only amplify the problem.

In my system, we tax on an Income vs. Effort scale. We create new tax brackets in which people with lower salaries are taxed at a much lower rate than those with huge salaries (say, for example, 20% for janitors vs. 40% for hedge fund managers). That's just the base rate. Your effort will determine your final tax rate. The more you work, the less you pay. If you work 80 hours a week, your tax rate drops in half. If you work 60 hours, your tax rate is 75%. If you work 20 hours a week, your tax rate doubles.

Here's the beauty of the plan: Most honest Americans

will end up paying about the same amount. Society's miscreants, on the other hand, will be punished. Someone who makes $5 million a year as a "producer" and spends all day sitting on a yacht, well that douchebag ends up with an 80% tax rate. He can't complain because he's still getting a million dollars a year to hit on models. Someone who got lucky on the stock market may be paying 70% in taxes, because they've made a bunch of money without contributing much to society. If someone makes a million dollars from a slip n' fall lawsuit, they pay 97% in taxes, because they're an idiot and they didn't do shit. But... if someone makes millions by working around the clock to form a start-up Internet company that employs a dozen people, their hard work is rewarded. They'll end up with a low tax rate, which is perfect because they work hard and create jobs. Their lower taxes are a thank you for making our country a better place.

(Note: People who inherit family money pay 65% in taxes, because even though they didn't do anything to earn that money per se, they still put up with their annoying family for 18 years.)

You might think this screws over part-time employees. Wrong. For starters, my plan contains a caveat that anyone currently in school pays a 10% tax rate. It sucks enough to get out of school and go to your job as a Stop 'N Shop cashier. We don't need to penalize kids any more. As for adults, well, part-time jobs pay crappy wages, so when you balance your abbreviated schedule with your low tax bracket, you don't end up paying too much. However, you don't make out like a bandit either. This inspires people to get better jobs without destroying their lives in the interim.

The idea is to create a system that rewards hard work and punishes laziness. People get to keep more of what they earn, but they also have to earn more of what they keep. It's incredibly fair for everyone.

Then, we kill all the old people and save on Medicare costs. That's right, we're coming after you, Grandpa.

Education

These days, everyone seems to be down on public schools, and in our usual rush to assign blame, we've focused on criticizing teachers. For some reason we think that bad teachers are the sole reason for public schools' lack of success. First off, I think it's necessary that we redefine our notion of success. Sorry, but some kids are dumb as rocks. The average graduation rate for public schools in America is roughly 70%. Considering all the dumb jocks and disinterested latchkey kids in our public school system, I don't think that's terrible. Of course that 70% figure means nothing because the rate for suburban schools is higher while the rate for deteriorating inner city schools is much lower. I won't understate the issue here. We have a problem with our public schools.

Now... I'm not an overly emotional individual. I don't care about too many issues. If a problem doesn't affect me personally, I'm unlikely to try and fix it. I don't get fired up often. I lack fulfilling personal relationships and deep down, I'm a vacuous shell of a man. However, I am passionate about one thing. I am sick and tired of hearing people blame educators for the decline in quality of our public schools. Some teachers are better than others, but none of them are the reason for the decline in our educational system. Teachers have, by far, the worst job in America. Worse than police, worse than janitors, and worse than the deep sea fishermen on "Deadliest Catch."

Teachers are paid next to nothing for what is the most stress-inducing job out there. Not only do they have to babysit a bunch of bratty, immature, crybaby, asshole kids, but they have to teach them about the War of 1812 while doing so. And if the kids don't learn enough, everyone blames the teachers. What about the fact that some kids are stupid? What about the fact that many children are, like I was, completely indifferent about their own success and prone to daydreaming? What about the fact that a lot of kids don't even show up to school in the first place? Educators are held responsible for a child's education even if said child never comes to school. It's ridiculous. Schools lose funding based on their graduation rates, and even a student that is truant the entire year counts against their statistics. Imagine if you were a basketball player, and you had to make a 3-point shot before a 24-second shot clock expired, except 15% of the time the ref refused to give you the ball. That's what it's like to be an educator. So you expel bad kids, or you give them a passing grade just to boost your numbers, but of course that flies in the face of everything we're trying to accomplish with our educational system.

Everyone points to summer vacations as a main reason why teachers shouldn't complain about their jobs. That's bullshit. Your kids get the entire summer off. Teachers don't. Teachers usually have to go back earlier than the students. They have to create lesson plans. They teach summer school, tutor, or take on additional summer jobs in order to make up for their lousy teacher salaries.

Teachers make personal sacrifices that none of us in the private sector could even imagine. For Christ's sake, they wake up at 6AM every morning. 6AM!!!

Someone needs to say it: The reason we have shitty students is because of shitty parents. Private schools aren't better because the teachers are better. They're better because the students come from wealthy families and have parents who care about their well-being. 98% of all kids are lazy no-good pains in the ass, but most still get an education because there's a parent making them do the legwork. If it were up to me I would have spent my childhood playing *Mortal Kombat* 14 hours a day and sleeping the other 12. I wouldn't have had any time for math. I would have fit eating in there somewhere, although "eating" means cramming Pop-Tarts down my throat while Scorpion did his finishing move on Sub-Zero. Luckily, because my parents cared about my future, they forced me to put down the SEGA controller, do homework, and participate in extracurricular activities. If I came from a broken home, or my father was an alcoholic, or my mother beat me with a frying pan, then I probably would have given up by age 13 and I'd be peddling meth in an alley right now instead of sitting in a nice office, pretending to do my job while writing this paragraph. So instead of bashing teachers, let's start blaming shitty parents for doing a shitty job and making our public schools such a shitty place for teachers to work.

Bathing Suit Mesh

That mesh lining they put inside all men's bathing suits is by far the most annoying thing on the planet. Forget about your cancer, poverty, and war. Bathing suit mesh is the worst. How can you design a men's bathing suit and not take into account the balls? It's really the only thing you should be considering. There's no need to restrain the balls. Unless your balls are two feet long, they're not going to hang out of the shorts or prohibit you from walking. Manufacturers should leave that region of the body alone as much as possible. Instead we get an army of invisible mesh fingers pushing our balls up against our taint. It's awful. The bathing suit only covers 15% of the male body, and somehow no one can get it right. That's why, whenever I buy a bathing suit, I immediately get scissors and cut out the mesh. It's simple, it takes two minutes to do, and yet it took me 25 years to figure this out. I implore you all to do the same. Your comfort will increase tenfold, and other beachgoers will be none the wiser.

Dating

Dating is tough. Young people are picky and strapped for time, making it very difficult to meet people. Online dating makes it easier to secure a date, but eventually you have to get together face-to-face with another human being, and chaos ensues. It's all a waste of time. The secret to dating or hook-up success is hanging out with people who are more attractive than you. It sounds counterintuitive but it works. For example, if you're an average-looking girl, you should find a group of really attractive girls and spend as much time as possible with them. Trust me. Average chicks are usually intimidated by hot chicks. It's stupid. They should cling to them like barnacles on the hull of a ship. They'll end up meeting way more guys that way. Sure, they won't get the top-tier guy, but the sheer amount of run-off they're exposed to will be amazing. This is the exact reason I hang out with Ashton Kutcher all the time. Well, that and his theories on gravitational time dilation.

Religion

Religion can inspire and teach values, but it can also leads to arguments and violence. Unfortunately, there's no chance of settling our religious differences. When you believe that one entity created the Earth and mankind, controlling everything, you'll fight to the death to defend that entity's teachings. That's why, starting with the next generation, we have to get everyone on the same religious page. We don't want anyone to feel left out, so we'll combine elements of every single religion into one uber-religion that we'll teach to all our future children. We'll work out the details, but basically with this uber-religion we'd all worship an invisible 8-armed fat guy with a sandals and a gray beard who teaches us to love one another and attain peace of mind while shooting anyone who disagrees with us. And just so the atheists are included, we'll make sure everyone says they believe in this uber-religion but then ignores its teachings in practice and does whatever they want instead. In other words, the uber-religion will be what 90% of the world practices already.

Racism

We've got a huge racial problem in this country, and I'm afraid it's not getting any better. That's right, I'm talking about white people trying to sing along to rap music. Back in the early '90s rappers made clean versions of their songs, also known as the "radio edit." Now, not only do they refuse to make an edited version of the track, but they've upped the number of n-words by 400%. As a white guy, how am I supposed to sing along to that? Oh sure, I can belt out a few "n****a pleases" in the comfort of my own home, but what about when I'm rolling in my '64 Impala and Tupac's "Hit 'Em Up" comes as I pull up next to a black guy at a red light? I can either turn down the greatest rap song of all-time, or a complete stranger will think I'm an asshole when he sees me screaming "y'all n****s can't be us or see us!!"

You black people just don't understand the plight of us white people who like rap. You can't comprehend what it's like to be a white rap fan in modern day America. It's tough out there. Oh, we say we've come a long way since the 1970s, but white people are still treated like second-class rap fans. Black people, you'll never understand.

You see, like Martin Luther King, Jr., I also have a dream. I dream of a world where black and white people can discuss the differences in races honestly, without resorting to hurtful stereotypes or pretending that everyone is exactly the same. I dream of a world where we can address social and racial issues openly, without fear of being called a racist by those who disagree with us. I dream of a world where white people can use the n-word, as long as they're quoting a historical figure or a rap song, and not using the term in a derogatory manner. I dream of a world where white and black people live together in the same neighborhood, the black people all have health insurance, and the white people don't have to purchase ADT Home Security Systems. That's my dream. Then, later in my dream, I have sex with Beyonce. You see, racial harmony can exist!

The Massive Decline in the Quality of Music That Has Occurred Since You Were a Teenager

Get an iPod.

Divorce

It's sad that we live in a society where divorce is so frequent. I hate all these couples who get divorced just because it's the trendy thing to do. They see their friends getting divorced, or they feel pressure from their parents and society, or refuse to bend from some ridiculous 5-year plan, and they get divorced even though they're too immature and not ready for that kind of commitment. It really makes a mockery out of the whole institution of divorce.

Nevertheless, with 60% of marriages ending in divorce, it's high time we started preparing for the unavoidable. If you were buying a house, you wouldn't spend every last penny you had on the down payment. You'd want money left over for renovations and unforeseen problems. The same should go for marriage. Figure out what it will cost you to get divorced, and then don't get married until you have at least 50% more than that number. That way, when divorce inevitably rears its ugly head, you'll have a nice cushion to fall back on. That's what we call smart financial planning. And forget about getting your engagement ring back. Some people believe a woman should return the engagement ring after a break-up, but to me, buying an engagement ring is like selling your kidney on the black market. Once it's gone, it's gone. Trust me, I know. Last year I gave my love an engagement ring and sold a kidney to the South Americans to get money for an iPhone, then tried getting them both back a month later when my fiancé fucked my best friend and I realized how high AT&T's service charges were. No luck on either front. Now I'm lovelorn and I'm pissing 25 times a day. Talk about buyer's remorse.

Assassinations

Every assassin throughout history has three names. John Wilkes Booth. Mark David Chapman. James Earl Ray. Lee Harvey Oswald. That's why the government has to step in and outlaw middle names. If all assassins have three names, and all future children only have two names, then via the transitive property no one can grow up to be an assassin. It's simple mathematics. And if that theory somehow fails, well, then, I guess we'll have to start loving our children.

Hangovers

Everyone claims to have a secret hangover cure, and none of these magical remedies ever work. Luckily for you, after many painful Sunday mornings, I have come up with a system that truly eliminates hangovers. This cure is the real deal, I promise you. First, sleep as long as you can. If you have to stay in bed until 3PM, do it. As soon as you wake up, immediately take two Advil. Not Tylenol, not Aleve, not generic Stop 'N Shop brand ibuprofen. Advil. Then, shower and wash away the smell of booze. A simple whiff of Jack Daniels can send you into a downward spiral the likes of which you are not prepared for. Now, drink three drinks simultaneously. One should be a massive container of water. The second drink should be a coffee. If you don't drink coffee, too bad, it's time to sack up and become a man. The third drink is Yellow Gatorade. That's the flavor Yellow, not the color yellow. Alternate sips of these three beverages while eating either a bread-based meal such as a large Subway sub, or greasy brunch-style food such as a ham and cheese omelet. Then, when you are exactly 62% done with your meal, pinch your nose, hold your breath for 30 seconds, then release your fingers, and immediately slam your face against a wall as hard as you can. Resume eating until you are finished. When you're done, sacrifice a baby goat and drink the blood straight from its neck. A goat from Eastern Europe works best, but if you can't find one of those, you can use a North American goat. In the event of a goat shortage, use a cat, but don't expect the same results. Once your throat is covered in the blood of this nubile animal, do 14 sit-ups while listening to the song "Butterfly" by Crazytown. Then, punch a pregnant woman in the stomach and dive onto the hood of a moving car. As you lie face-up on the asphalt, stare straight into the sun and scream "FREEDOM!" at the top of your lungs. Finally, scrape yourself up off of the road, crawl back inside, and immediately pound 10 beers. Why? Because there's no such thing as a hangover cure, you fucking idiot, but you can't be hungover if you never stop drinking.

The Younger Generation

"Kids these days." Baby boomers are always ripping on my generation, calling us lazy, apathetic, and constantly distracted. Hey, old fucks, the reason this generation is always distracted is because we keep on inventing awesome new things to distract us. Congratulations on making slight improvements to the automobile over 40 years and adding a clock to a toaster oven. My generation invented 8,000 new web apps *today*. We also found a way to connect people everywhere and create a world without borders. But hey, I know, you were at Woodstock, man. All you baby boomers who are disgusted by this generation, you can go fellate yourself. I know that's impossible, but don't worry, my generation will figure it out soon.

Free Will vs. Determinism

Some people believe that everything happens for a reason, or that there's some master plan behind all of this. I happen to think life is more like a game of poker. The people who practice, accumulate knowledge, and play the game the right way often succeed, but sometimes you just get dealt a terrible hand. When that happens, you can either fold and give up, or push your chips into the pile and go for broke, but no matter how hard you try, sometimes you get a bad card on the river, and then you either have to go fish or pray for a blackjack, and if the little metal ball doesn't land on red, well then… alright, I'll be honest, I have no idea how to play poker. I was just trying to impress you guys. I'm sorry.

Stupidity

You can't fix stupid. However, you can trick it easily. So let's start tricking stupid people into giving us all of their money. That way we'll be rich and stupid people will have to live in a cheaper area, far away from us smart folks. I know that seems mean, but really we're just giving Darwinism a push in the right direction.

AIDS

Don't get AIDS.

Global Warming

There are two stances on global warming. People on the "left" believe global warming is a huge problem and one of the biggest threats to the survival of our planet. People on the "right" deny that global warming is happening. I have a third stance. I believe in global warming, and I'm all for it. As I'm writing this, it's the middle of winter, and it sucks. It's freezing and I have to wake up 20 minutes early every morning to shovel out my car. I don't want to move out of the Northeast because my family is here, but I also would like to experience the kind of tropical climate they have in Miami. So let's keep this global warming thing afloat, literally. Some people say that global warming will flood the country and submerge major cities. I say, it will create more beaches. Hey, I'm a glass-half-full kind of guy.

My only wish is that more global warming deniers would acknowledge that human activity is detrimental to our atmosphere and admit that they don't care. It's fine. You won't get any judgment from me. I'll be long dead before the fossil fuels run out so why should I give a fuck? Let our kids figure that out. It'll give them something to do after their 807th game of *Call of Duty*.

We should recycle. We should turn off lights and appliances when we're not using them. We shouldn't litter. These are basic solutions that I think most people can get behind. But we're not going to give up our cars to stop some world destruction that could be millenniums in the future. Call that appalling, but at this moment in time the general public is too dependent on gasoline and other chemicals and it's nearly impossible to make the drastic life changes required to reverse humans' impact on the Earth. We're not going to get rid of cars. Public transportation is unreliable and it never takes you close enough to where you need to go. Riding a bike sounds like a great idea, except everyone else is driving an SUV the size of a school bus, and you *will* die if you try to pedal a Huffy down a major road. Using cloth grocery bags sounds like a good idea, but I've tried to suffocate small children with those things and it's just not the same. Reducing aerosol cans is another thing that makes sense on paper, but man, fuck that shit, I gotta look good.

One compromise is to buy a hybrid or electric car, but have you seen the prices on those things? I'm supposed to pay extra to save the environment? Fuck that. They say that necessity is the mother of invention. Well, I guess that means every time I fill my gas tank I'm the father of invention. If I go green, I'm really just being an absentee dad, and that's irresponsible. If the government really wanted us to reduce our carbon footprint, they would offer massive incentives for everyone who bought hybrid cars and used cloth grocery bags. Instead they tax manufacturers of forward-thinking products and allow companies that don't give a shit about the environment to make millions by profiting on bogus "green" marketing campaigns.

I say fuck the planet. Clearly the planet is out to get us. There are tornados, earthquakes, monsoons, and according to scientists, the temperature of the Earth is rising at a rate that will eventually kill the entire species. We can't just sit there and take that shit. We need to fight back. The Earth is trying to kill us, so we have to kill it first. On the other hand, it's actually easier to reduce your carbon footprint than it is to destroy the

Earth. Littering takes more effort than not littering. Turning off the lights requires the flick of a switch, which is easier than writing all those extra zeros on your monthly electric bill if you decide to leave the lights on. And throwing something in a recycling bin is the exact same effort as throwing something in the trash. Since my laziness supersedes my disdain for the planet Earth and its murderous ways, I say let's try this conservation thing for the next 50 years or so. And if that doesn't work, well then it's game on, Earth — get ready to die!

Everything Else

…or we could just have child licenses. Make no mistake, all of the world's problems are a direct result of overpopulation. When you see a starving child in Africa, an angry terrorist in the Middle East, or a crack baby in Kansas City, know that those people ended up where they are because there simply weren't enough resources on this planet to go around. How come global warming is this big issue now but nobody mentioned climate change in 1930? It's because there are twice as many people on Earth today polluting. Why does our government have to charge such high taxes? To provide roads, schools, homeless shelters, food stamps, and welfare for the 380 million people in this country. Human beings are highly-evolved animals, but we're still animals, and we fuck accordingly. People around the world have no problem procreating without thinking about the consequences. It's insane that we require people to get licenses for duck hunting but not for bringing a human into the planet. Children that are poorly cared for grow up to be the root of all of the world's problems. They are the murderers, rapists, and home invaders of our society. Girls who are born to uncaring mothers grow up to have an uncared for litter of their own, and as the cycle continues, our problems intensify. The only benefit of bad parenting is that it brings us a surplus of strippers, and although I think we can all agree that strippers rock, the bonus of plentiful lap dances doesn't outweigh all of the negatives brought upon us by the scorned youth of the world.

Here's how child licenses would work. Before you conceive a child, you must first obtain a license. You would need a separate license for every child you have. To get a license, you would have to pass a series of tests. The most important test would be proving that you can provide for a child. There would be a credit check and a background check. It would be similar to the process you go through when renting an apartment or buying a car. Why is it that we can require proof of income to buy a $8,000 used Hyundai, but kids cost hundreds of thousands of dollars and you can have as many as you want? There should also be a psychiatric evaluation. Again, nothing too intense, just a simple test to make sure the potential parents aren't completely crazy. Simply going through the effort to obtain the license would prove that you cared about the welfare of your future child, at least a little bit. That would easily put you ahead of 15% of current parents.

Speaking of welfare, anyone who has a child without first obtaining a license will lose 50% of their future government benefits. When it comes to unemployment or welfare, you can only get half as much as everyone else. If a President decides to send everyone a $600 check like George Bush did that one time, you get $300. If you have two children without a license, you are cut off completely. There will be no mandated abortion and no child will ever be taken away simply because the parents failed to obtain a license. You will just never get anything from the government, ever. All of the money you would have received through welfare or handouts will be put into a fund that we will use for legal fees when your child eventually grows up and shoots a cashier at the 7-Eleven.

This plan will vastly decrease the number of problem children, and since problem children cause problems, ergo it will drastically decrease the number of problems facing our country. It will cut down on crime and add billions to our budget. It's the perfect plan, really.

Of course it will never happen, so my suggestion to everyone is to take a shuttle to the moon and start from scratch over there.

36
The Meaning of Life, Part VI

Umm…

…

yeah…

…

…

I got nothing.

37
Take This Seriously

I'm writing this on a Friday.

On Monday, I'll be in the hospital, with a tube inserted into my heart.

About three months ago, I was sitting at work when I suddenly began having chest pain. It started with a minor discomfort in the sternum, lightheadedness, and a strange feeling in my arms. Over the next ten minutes, it escalated into an intense pain. My chest was so tight I could barely breathe. I thought I was having a heart attack. It was by far the most excruciating pain I've ever experienced. I made my way over to a coworker, who called 911. Soon I was in the hospital, where after hours of tests, doctors determined that I did not have a heart attack. After confirming that my life was not in immediate danger, doctors discharged me from the emergency room.

Now, after months of doctors' appointments, procedures and blood work, my cardiologist discovered that my heart wasn't functioning to its full capacity. The medical term is cardiomyopathy. I'm no expert, but based on the small amount of his medical jargon that I was able to translate to English, my heart is pumping at roughly two-thirds the strength of a normal heart. That's why, on Monday, I'll be undergoing a procedure called an angiogram to see if there are any blockages in my heart or major arteries. The doctors will insert a tube into my femoral artery that they will then feed up to my heart. This will allow them to view the inside of my heart on a computer screen. I've been assured that this is relatively safe as far as cardiac procedures go. Then again, I'm a fan of the show "Dexter," and I know that the Trinity Killer murdered his victims by slicing open the femoral artery, so the fact that someone is going to make an incision into my femoral artery on purpose isn't very comforting.

There's a good chance the doctors who perform the procedure on Monday won't find any blockage. I'm sure that if this was a true medical emergency, I wouldn't be waiting 5 days to have the procedure done. I'd have my testicles hanging out of a hospital gown right now. Of course, even sound logic like that is of little comfort when you're about to have a tube jammed up your groin. They're also going to shave my pubic hair before the surgery, which is kind of freaking me out. I haven't read *GQ Magazine* lately but I'm pretty sure the 8-year old boy look is not one of their Hot Summer Fashion Tips.

My cardiologist believes that a virus devastated my heart muscles and thus my ability to pump blood throughout my body. He thinks the virus is now gone, based on my slight improvement over the past several weeks. Right now it's all speculation. If the angiogram turns up nothing, then my heart will be deemed safe and I'll take medication to try and fix the damage done by this alleged virus. I'll also have to undergo another series of procedures to make sure that nothing else is wrong. So while I'll probably end up fine, I'll also most likely spend the next 6 months taking various pills and spending most of my time on the couch.

It's been a rough ride. Any physical or emotional exertion currently results in more chest pain, making it tough to do anything. I can't go out with my friends, unless we're sitting around at someone's house. Even then it's tough. I can't drink at all. Forget about physical activity. I'm an avid skier and golfer, but I had to cut this ski season short, and I probably won't be able to go golfing at all this summer. I used to go to the gym three or four times a week. That's done. I love the outdoors and I usually have a very active social life. All of that has been curtailed by my health issues. It's been difficult, to say the least. What do people who don't drink and don't do physical activity do all day? I know people like that exist, but I have no clue how they spend their time. Do I need to buy an Xbox? Maybe I need to pick up a hobby that doesn't involve exertion, like model ship building or Satan worship.

When all is said and done, my 2011 will essentially be a wasted year. These medical problems didn't kill me, but they've definitely ruined my life for the time being. I've lost 33 pounds due to a combination of stress and an inability to eat full meals. I weighed 178 lbs. to begin with, so now I resemble a starving Ethiopian child. I can't begin to express how frustrating the past three months have been. The non-stop tests and appointments, the quest to find doctors who weren't rushing me out of the room, the thousands in medical bills; it's been a nightmare. The worst part, by far, is the waiting. Not knowing what's wrong and searching for an answer to this illness has been eternally annoying.

For 30 years, I've prided myself on living in the moment and enjoying life as much as possible.

Right now, my life sucks.

This is the final chapter of the book. By this point, assuming you haven't skipped half the chapters, you've read dozens of jokes about gay people. There have been plenty of jokes about race. I've mocked many musicians and celebrities. There were insults about potheads, alcoholics, Internet addicts, Presidents, terrorists, strippers, hot dog vendors, rich people, poor people, fat people, stupid people, and kids. I poked fun at religion a few times. You've witnessed several rape jokes and a couple of pleas to kill old people. Yes, I've even made a few jokes about diseases.

None of it matters.

The truth is, there are not a lot of things that are important in life. To me, the list includes family, friends, and especially now, health. I'd probably include the band Pearl Jam on that list as well, but that's just me. I'm sure every individual has a few other things they'd add. But if you live in America, you're healthy, you have loving friends and family, and you make enough to pay the bills, then you already have everything you need, whether you know it or not.

So let's not get offended by jokes. For the record, I'm straight, but I have some very close gay friends and I envy the gay lifestyle (minus the gay sex part). I'm anti-rape. I love all types of music, including most of the artists I've made fun of in this book. I appreciate the work of strippers. I like kids. I don't want to murder the elderly. And I don't think it's funny when someone gets AIDS, although I do find AIDS jokes hilarious.

I don't know what's going on in our country, but these days it seems like everyone has their panties in a bunch. Maybe it's the recession, or the abundance of negative imagery we see on TV every day. Whatever the cause, it seems like everyone is offended by everything. It's one thing to get angry at politicians for illegal or immoral activity, but nowadays we're even getting mad at comedians for telling jokes. The amount of offended individual and groups, as well as the quantity of vitriol spewed by the offended, has grown steadily in the past decade. We've become a nation of angry, uptight, easily-offended spazzes.

So before we say goodbye, I'd like to offer a final plea. Please, everyone, can we get a perspective and realize what's important? My health problems have been a major burden, but they're still trivial compared to the millions of people worldwide who battle terminal diseases. There's a 10% unemployment rate in America. Starvation runs rampant across the globe. Young women are being sold as sex slaves. People are working shitty jobs for their entire lives, and when they turn 65, they still don't have enough money to retire. Let's start taking these issues seriously, and let's start treating jokes as jokes. Even if the jokes happen to be about these very issues. A joke never hurt anyone. Don't get me wrong, words can occasionally hurt. When the "God Hates Fags" church members protest a soldier's funeral, that's extremely hurtful, because those assholes' actions are inhibiting the rights and liberties of others. But when someone makes a passing joke about a gay pride parade, that doesn't have any effect, because it's a joke and the person isn't actually doing anything to anyone. It may have hurt your feelings, but if there's one lesson everyone needs to learn about life, it's that no one cares about your feelings. So shut up. You don't have to get offended to prove you care about something. You're not doing anyone (or any group) any favors by being offended on their behalf. Usually you just make everyone hate that person or group even more. As children, we learn that actions speak louder than words, yet as adults we put way too much stock in words while often ignoring actions. And let's remember that you have to be in a position of comfort to even be offended by a joke in the first place. You know who isn't offended by jokes about African children? African children. They're busy trying to eat.

Personally I don't care about anything, but I can understand why people get upset over injustice and social inequalities. I'll never understand how someone could be offended by a joke. A joke is not an action. It's just a word. It's something that never actually happened. Like the Holocaust.

This planet will still be spinning long after we're all gone. In the grand scheme of things, nobody's life is that important. Our most cherished leaders are eventually resigned to the back pages of history and the average person's life matters to only a select few. We're all going to die sooner or later. So you might as well loosen up and have a little fun.

I guess what I'm trying to say is, if you're offended by anything I wrote in this book, then fuck you.

Everyone else, thanks for reading!

The Mothafuckin' End.

This book is dedicated to Rachael Walsh, Chris Davis, Tori Pugliese, and America.

About the Author

Tom Z was born in Boston, but he grew up in Syracuse, NY. It worked out well because with his slow Upstate drawl he can say inappropriate things and people will laugh, whereas with a Boston accent he'd sound like a total dick. When he graduated high school, there was a thunderous applause, not because anyone cared about him, but because his name starts with a Z, so he was last and everyone was glad the boring ceremony was over. Tom's interests include '90s rock, mesh shorts, hot dogs, sleep, flannel shirts, the Buffalo Bills, getting drunk on Sundays, unironically listening to R. Kelly, and most importantly, writing. OK, that's a lie, writing is like 9th on that list. It's WAY behind Sunday Funday. His dislikes include grocery shopping, the band Aerosmith and any show on the Bravo channel. Tom lives his life by one simple motto: "Maximum results with minimal effort." He's willing to put in the work to achieve his goals, but he'd prefer those goals fall into his lap without any effort. He currently lives in Connecticut and has an Asian girlfriend, which he believes entitles him to make all the racist jokes he wants. He insults her driving, but she took his soul, so they're even. That's about it. Oh, and also, this one time he went out to the bar wearing 8 popped collars. It was pretty funny.

The Meaning of Life
(and AIDS Jokes)

By Tom Z
www.thetomzshow.com

Published by Tom Z Industries
ISBN# 978-0-9846973-0-4

www.ingramcontent.com/pod-product-compliance
Lightning Source LLC
Chambersburg PA
CBHW071452040426
42444CB00008B/1307